How To Speak the Word of God with the Voice of Jesus

Jesus is Lord
Ivoryiett Jones
4866 North 48th Street
Milwaukee, WI 53

How To Speak the Word of God with the Voice of Jesus

Dr. Leroy Thompson Sr.

EVER INCREASING
Acts 6:7
WORD
MINISTRIES
Darrow, La.
WORD OF LIFE CHRISTIAN CENTER

Unless otherwise indicated, all Scripture quotations in this volume are from the *King James Version* of the Bible.

First Printing 1998

ISBN 0-963-2584-2-7

Ever Increasing Word Ministries
P.O. Box 7
Darrow, Louisiana 70725

Contents

Preface

The part of the Bible that will produce results for you is the part that is real to you in your spirit and that you speak out with a *voice* and not just an *echo*.

What we have to do is find out the difference between a voice and an echo. In my more than twenty years of ministry, I have seen a lot of "parakeeting" of the Word of God. In other words, people have just been repeating or echoing what they heard somebody else say or what they read out of a book. But what they heard or read never became real to them. They were just an echo, not a voice. The Word never produced anything for them because they did not give the Holy Spirit time to work it in them — to reveal and unfold it to them so they could use *personally* what God was saying to them from His Word.

An echo is empty. It has no power or authority, and it produces no results. Many believers know the Scriptures. They speak them for healing, finances, happy family relationships, long life, and so forth. But they seem always to be waiting for answers and manifestations. They've resigned themselves to waiting; they've come to *expect* having to wait!

There is an answer to this problem, and that's what I want to talk about in this book. I believe that when you learn to speak the Word of God with the voice of Jesus, you can have the same power Jesus had and receive the same results Jesus received when He was on the earth.

I appreciate the Lord opening up His Word to His people. What an advantage we have in life when we understand how to take the Word of God into our situations and experience victory.

Chapter 1
The Power of the Abiding Word

If ye abide in me, and MY WORDS ABIDE IN YOU,
ye shall ask what ye will, and it shall be done unto you.

— John 15:7

In this book, I'm going to show you why you may have been making some confessions yet have not gotten any manifestations. Largely, it is because you've been taking the Bible as something you know you're supposed to quote, confess, and speak out, but it has not become real to you like it should have.

It takes *time* for the Word of God to become real to you. But when the Word becomes revelation to you personally, you are going to increase in life! You will increase in your love walk, your relationships, your home, your money, your healing, and everything that concerns you. Why? Because of the power of the Word when it is made real and personal to you.

The Father's intent was that we get the same results from the Word that Jesus got. Jesus spoke to the wind, telling it to cease, and the wind said, "Okay" (Mark 4:39). He spoke to the raging waters, and the water said, "I'll obey you" (Mark 4:39; Luke 8:24). Jesus spoke to the fig tree. He said, "Go ahead and die." The fig tree said to the roots, "Let's die!" And the fig tree died (Matt. 21:19; Mark 11:14, 20). Jesus did all that through the power of the Word.

In this chapter, I want to share with you something God has dealt with me about, and that is *the power of the abiding Word.* To do that, I need to talk about the power of the *rhema*

1

word and what power exists and is available when you have a "rhema word" from God.

A 'Rhema Word' Defined

You might ask, "Brother Thompson, what is a 'rhema word'?" Well, "rhema" is a Greek word meaning *the word spoken*. When I use the phrase "rhema word," I am referring to the spoken Word of God or a *quickened* word from God.

A rhema word is a word that is actually alive in your inner man — your spirit — and it is beyond your "head" or intellect. It is a word from God that is beyond your memorization. In other words, a rhema word is an abiding word, and there's *power* in the abiding Word of God!

I've had some "rhemas" spoken to me over the years that have blessed me tremendously. It is a blessing when everything looks wrong, but you know that it is all going to be all right! Whatever God has spoken to you may look like it's not going to come to pass, but you know what God has said and that it is going to happen, because you have a rhema word!

The rhema word is that which is spoken. It is a word, a promise, or an individual scripture that the Holy Spirit brings to your remembrance in the time of need. It is a word spoken by God, and it is a word spoken directly to you for a particular situation.

Have you ever been reading the Bible and, all of a sudden, one individual scripture just "leaps" out of the Bible on you? The second it does, revelation just starts rolling! You feel as if you could solve your whole life's situations with that one scripture!

That's when God is talking directly to you. Within that rhema word is enough power to make it come to pass instantly in you, because it went down into you, into your spirit.

The Holy Spirit brings a rhema word to our remembrance

in our time of need. But that doesn't just happen every day. We have a part to play. We have to abide in the Word of God.

It takes some effort to get to that place of confidence with God. When you dig into the Word of God, it can become so much a part of you that you can know beyond a shadow of a doubt that what God said, He is able to perform!

As I said, when a rhema word comes to you from God, the power to bring that word to pass is already contained within it. When God reveals Himself to you in this way from His Word, all you need to do is simply accept it, act on it, and trust in Him to bring it to pass.

The main way you receive a rhema word is by meditating on the Word, abiding in it, and letting it abide in you. There are some things that will try to keep the Word from abiding in you. Why? Because once the Word of God begins to abide in you and it becomes a rhema word — a word from God spoken directly to you — then when you "talk" that word or speak it, situations change immediately!

It's like when Jesus talked to the fig tree in Matthew 21.

MATTHEW 21:19
19 And when he [Jesus] saw a fig tree in the way, he came to it, and found nothing thereon, but leaves only, and said unto it, Let no fruit grow on thee henceforward for ever. And PRESENTLY the fig tree withered away.

There is a way to cause the Word of God to abide in you, and when that Word abides in you, it will produce a certain power. Our text says, *"If ye abide in me, and my words abide in you, YE SHALL ASK WHAT YE WILL, AND IT SHALL BE DONE UNTO YOU"* (John 15:7). That is the power of the abiding Word!

The Promises of God Are *Conditional*

What did Jesus say? He said, *". . . ask what ye will, and it shall be done unto you."* He also said, *"If you abide in Me, and*

My words abide in you. . . ." So, first, we must recognize that
the promise "ask whatever you will, and it shall be done unto
you" is *conditional*. When *"if"* is the first word you see in a
verse, then you know the promise of that verse is conditional!
In other words, your receiving the promise depends on your
doing your part and meeting the conditions of the promise.

In John 15:7, there are certain conditions you have to
fulfill in order to be able to "ask whatever you will." What are
the conditions? It says you have to abide in Jesus and His
words have to abide in you.

Also, there are certain conditions you have to fulfill to get
Jesus' words to abide in you in the first place. One of those
conditions is, the Word of God must be personal to *you*.

The Promises of God Are *Personal*

We know John 15:7 and the promise of "asking whatever
you will" is conditional. But it is also *personal*. It's not a
corporate or group proposition. You, *individually* will have to
make every effort to cause the Word to abide in you.

I want you to notice five personal pronouns in John 15:7.

JOHN 15:7
**7 If YE abide in me, and my words abide in YOU, YE shall
ask what YE will, and it shall be done unto YOU.**

In other words, the word "you" or "ye" is used five times
in that one verse! Actually, if you'll study the entire context
from verses 7 through 11, you will find some form of the word
"you" there more than ten times. You see, there's a God-ward
side and a man-ward side to receiving from God. We think
God is going to do everything, but there's a part we have to
play in order for God to do something for us.

You have a part to play. There are many instances of the
word "you" in those verses and several instances of the word
"abide." So, you see, the only power of the Word that *you* will
experience is the power of the Word that's *abiding* in *you*! It's
not the power of the Word abiding in your neighbor, brother,

sister, pastor, or fellow church member that will benefit you. No, it's the Word abiding in *you* that will produce power in your own life.

A lot of times we want to read a scripture and leave it up to God to fulfill it in our lives. But through His great plan of redemption, which included Jesus' death, burial, and resurrection, God has already done all He is going to do for us! Now it is our part — the responsibility is on us — to take the Word of God, obtain revelation knowledge, and operate in the faith and authority that really belong to us as children of God.

Actually, the power of God that you experience in life is more up to you than it is up to the Lord. It's your assignment to make sure that you have the Word abiding in you.

How To Get the Word To Abide in You

In order for the Word of God to become revelation to you, the Word has to abide in you. I'm going to show you how to get the word to *abide*.

JOHN 15:7
7 If ye ABIDE in me, and my words ABIDE in you, ye shall ask what ye will, and it shall be done unto you.

The word "abide" in this scripture means *to remain*. And the reason the Word has to *remain* in you is, you have a "spiritual digestive system" inside of you. The spiritual realm runs parallel with the natural realm, so just as your physical man has a digestive system that digests *physical* or *natural* food, your spirit man has a digestive system that digests *spiritual* food — the Word of God.

Spiritual Food Can Build a Strong Spirit And Make Your Words Creative!

When you eat physical food, it takes time for that food to go to different parts of your body to serve you with the necessary nutrients for physical life and health.

Well, in the spiritual realm, it's the same way. When you feed your spirit man with the Word of God, that Word becomes food and nutrition for your spirit. But it has to stay in your spirit long enough to become "digested." That Word has to stay in your spirit long enough to cause the life and power in that Word — the anointing — to abide in you in such a way that when you speak that Word out again, it will become a sword of the Spirit that will cut through circumstances and cause things to come to pass that couldn't have happened any other way. (I'll talk in detail about the sword of the Spirit in another chapter.)

Actually, when your words come out of your spirit or heart as a revelation from God, your words become *creative words*. What do I mean by "a revelation from God"? I mean, a word spoken to *you* or, in other words, a rhema. You see, it's a personal thing.

We know that the Word of God is spiritual food. Matthew 4:4 says, "*...Man shall not live by bread alone, but by every word that proceedeth out of the mouth of God.*" We do not live by bread (physical food) alone but by every word that proceeds from the mouth of God (spiritual food).

Man is more than a physical man. He *is* a spirit; he *has* a soul; and he *lives in* a body (1 Thess. 5:23). So he can't just live on physical food, because he's more than just a physical man. He has to have spiritual food too. His spirit man will have to feed on the Word of God in order to survive and be satisfied spiritually.

You know, some Christians try to make every kind of thing you can think of work for them when they have a need in their lives. They put their trust in all kinds of natural things that they hope will help them. They hope in spiritual things, too, such as the gifts of the Spirit, to see if they can receive a manifestation. That's good, but the gifts of the Spirit operate as the *Spirit* wills, not as *man* wills (1 Cor. 12:11).

Build a Solid Faith-Life
On the Word, Not on Spiritual Gifts

I thank God for the gifts of the Spirit, but, friend, we need to concentrate on the Word of God, not only on spiritual gifts. Why? Because the gifts of the Spirit may not manifest today, and they may not show up tomorrow, either, because they are manifested as the *Spirit* wills. *But the Word of God is always the same.* It is unchanging, and it is available to you today — *right now!*

You need to become a student of the Word until you become matured in the Word. When you are matured in the Word, the first thing you reach for when opposition comes is your sword — the sword of the Spirit! And you know beyond a shadow of a doubt that your sword will not fail you! Why? Because it is the unchanging Word of God that you've allowed to abide deep within your spirit. No matter how you feel, how the situation looks, or what others say, you "know that you know" that God's Word is sure and that it has the power to bring to pass in your life what God has said!

I want to get across to you that abiding in the Word is a personal thing. It's something you have to do for yourself. You can belong to a church, attend faithfully, take notes, and sing and shout out loud! But until you become a student of the Word, you will not be able to take the sword of the Spirit and "cut down" your circumstances and deal wisely in the affairs of life.

You need to understand that in every adverse situation in life, God will give you a "live" word from Heaven, a quickened word, that you can use as a sword to cut that situation down. That's why He sent His Word — so we could deal wisely in the affairs of life and make the affairs of life obey us.

Why Many Christians Are Defeated

We've seen that man should not live by bread alone but by every word that proceedeth out of the mouth of God (Matt. 4:4). And we know that there is power in the Word. I want to ask you a question. With all this power available, *why are so many Christians defeated?* They are defeated because they do not have the Word *abiding* in them. That's where the difference lies. When the Word is abiding in us, we are feeding on it and trusting it to bring the answer to pass. And that Word works, because it is *abiding.*

I think what has happened to cause many to fail is, they are in good churches, all right, but they are just "pronouncing" or enunciating slogans and words that they've heard *others* speak. They don't really have the Word abiding in them to the extent that it becomes power in them that produces results when *they* speak.

For example, God gave me a rhema word on money to share with the Body of Christ. He gave me the words "Money cometh," and those words have revolutionized my life and the lives of many others. But to many people, those words are not "rhema"; they are just a slogan. I was praying before a meeting I held recently in Miami, Florida, and the Lord told me that "Money cometh" is not a *slogan* but a *solution.* It is a solution to the financial problems that many are facing in the Body of Christ.

This is the reason why I do not endorse or permit others to produce any T-shirts, bumper stickers, badges, pins, and so forth, using the words "Money cometh." These paraphernalia tend to turn the words "Money cometh" from a prophetic word into just a slogan. The phrase "Money cometh" is catchy. People "pick up on it" and say it without the revelation, and it becomes mere commonplace words. But "Money cometh" is much more than that. It's a solution to people's financial distress.

Look at John 15:7 again: *"If ye abide in me, and my words abide in you, ye shall ask what ye will, and it shall be done unto you."* Look at that phrase ". . . *ask what YE WILL . . ."* Does God mean what He says? Yes, He does! You see, when you meditate on the Word of God and stay with it until it begins talking back to you personally about your situation, then your will becomes God's will. God's Word is His will, so as you let the Word abide in you, God actually plants His will in you. Then you have something in your spirit to talk to Him about so He can agree with you and bring to pass what you are talking to Him about.

God's Word Can Make You Stalwart and Confident!

When you pray about a situation, if you have a "live" or living word in your spirit concerning what belongs to you, then you won't come out of your prayer closet empty-handed. You'll come out with the answer! That's why John said in First John 5:14, ". . . *this is the confidence that we have in him, that, if we ask any thing according to his will, he heareth us."*

This is the confidence. You see, when you have a word from God — when the Word of God is abiding in your spirit — you live, move, walk, talk, sing, pray, ask questions, and give answers with confidence! The Word of God produces confidence in you. Even though life's circumstances may be coming at you, and the wind of adversity is blowing hard in one direction, you have the power of the abiding Word. You have the wind of the Holy Ghost — the anointing that's on the abiding Word — that can blow that wind of adversity back where it came from!

There's life in the Word, and that life produces confidence in you. With that kind of confidence, even before your circumstances change, you'll know you're the winner. You will see yourself winning.

When we pray in faith according to God's will, we have confidence. Well, how do we ask things according to His will? We go back to John 15:7: *"If ye abide in me, and my words abide in you, ye shall ask what ye will, and it shall be done unto you."* If we are abiding in the Word, we can pray the Word and know with confidence that we're praying properly. We know that God must answer, because He cannot turn His back on His Word. God and His Word are one, and God cannot deny Himself.

Jesus and the Word are one, so when you are praying the Word, He has to step up and say, "He's talking about Me. I've got to do it."

But before you can pray the Word in faith, you have to *know* the Word. You have to be acquainted with it in your spirit, not just in your head. You have to *know that you know!* You can't be really abiding and be "in and out" and wishy-washy about what you believe. The only way you are going to be steady and sturdy and confident is if you are abiding or remaining in the Word consistently.

The Power of Agreeing With God!

I want to talk more about the creative language of God. The creative language of God is demonstrated when you speak forth the creative Word of God in boldness and confidence because it is abiding in your spirit.

You remember the story of the tower of Babel in Genesis chapter 11. The people were in agreement together; they were of one mind and language, and the Lord said they couldn't be stopped. They would be successful at carrying out whatever they planned to do.

Well, when you speak the language of God from your heart, you are agreeing with God, and nothing shall be impossible to you! Nobody can stop the language of God. Why? Because God's words are *creative.* They are full of life and power! And they will be full of life and power to *you* if you will let those words abide in you!

Reasons Why the Word
Doesn't Abide in a Believer

Now what causes the Word *not* to abide in a believer? Well, one reason is that there is an enemy, and he comes to steal the Word before it can be productive in your spirit and in your life. John 10:10 says, *"The thief* [the enemy, the devil] *cometh not, but for to steal, and to kill, and to destroy: I am come that they might have life, and that they might have it more abundantly."* The main thing the thief wants to steal is the Word. If he can steal the Word from you, he's got your health; he's got your wealth; he's got your happy family relationships. If Satan can steal the Word from your heart, he's got your obedience — your submission to God's Word and will. The enemy steals everything when he steals God's Word from you.

There are many reasons why the enemy can steal the Word from a believer. One of the main reasons he can steal it is that the believer doesn't really understand it. In other words, the believer is not walking in the light of it, because he's not meditating on the Word and letting it abide in his heart or spirit like he should.

For example, some people are not loving and forgiving toward others, and the devil uses that against them. Ephesians 4:32 says, *"And be ye kind one to another, tenderhearted, forgiving one another, even as God for Christ's sake hath forgiven you."*

I always exhort married folks to just "take the low seat" when it comes to dealing with their spouses. Do you know what I mean by "taking the low seat"? I mean, be ye kind to one another, tenderhearted, forgiving one another!

You see, a husband and wife are the most powerful team that exists, and the enemy is always trying to make husbands and wives be at odds with one another. He tries to get them to "rub each other the wrong way" and to fight about any little thing that comes up. You've got to recognize and catch that. You've got to know who the enemy is and how he operates, because he knows how powerful you are together. As a husband and wife, if both of you are believers and are in agreement according to the Word, all things can become possible to you, and the devil doesn't want that to happen!

So take the low seat and be kind, tenderhearted, and loving toward one another. Smith Wigglesworth said he believed many were sick in the Body of Christ as a result of one or more of three things: *hard-heartedness*; a *critical, fault-finding spirit*; and *unforgiveness*.

Rev. Kenneth E. Hagin often tells of an elderly man he once knew who in his nineties still had all his hair, his teeth, his strength, and even his sex life with his wife! He told Brother Hagin, "It's because I've kept *this* over the years," and he held out his tongue. He kept his tongue — his mouth — from sinning.

Many people don't realize the power of the tongue or the power of confession and what it can do to you and for you, both positive and negative. Most people say things that aren't right because they don't feel good physically, or they are being moved or oppressed by circumstances. But that's not the time to be mean and nasty. That's the time to keep quiet and only say what you want to come to pass.

I'll talk more later about the power of confession, but let me exhort you: Don't say anything that you don't want to come to pass! Satan will try to cause that which you say that's negative to come to pass. Sometimes, he can take your *negative* confession and bring it to pass quicker than God can bring to pass your *positive* confession. Why? Because you've been programmed so long to think and talk negatively. You have to make the effort to renew your mind and change your way of thinking to line up with the Word of God. When you do, and the Word in you becomes a revelation — a rhema word — life will be different for you!

HEBREWS 2:1
1 Therefore we ought to give the more earnest heed to the
things which we have heard, lest at any time we should let
them slip.

Hebrews 2:1 exhorts us not to let the Word slip. You see,
we can get excited about the Word in a meeting. But later, we
don't always keep confessing and pumping that same Word
into our hearts that caused us to get excited at the meeting.
We don't continue putting pressure on the Word for it to bring
to pass what we heard at the meeting that made us so happy!

You see, if we will be consistent with it, the Word will
cause what we shout about to be manifested in our lives.
Remember what Jesus said, *"If ye abide in me, and my words
abide in you, ye shall ask what ye will, and it shall be done
unto you"* (John 15:7). Jesus said, "Ask what ye will, and the
Word will put you in a position to receive it."

The Lord said, in essence, "Call on Me, and I'll answer
you while you're calling." You see, the Word will put you in a
position that anything you ask the Lord for, or anything that
you speak according to the Word, will be manifested —
sometimes *instantly.*

I've put into practice these truths that I'm sharing with
you. I've come to the point in my faith life where I just *think*
about certain things, and they just show up! I don't even *say*
a lot of those things; I just *think* them. Maybe somewhere
down the line, I made my confession, because you do have to
speak out God's Word that you have in your heart. You have
to confess what you believe. But I've been getting to the point
where I really have to be mindful of what I *think,* because
those things can just show up at my house!

These things happen when you train your recreated
human spirit to meditate and abide in the Word and to think
consistently in line with God's Word.

Abiding means more than just taking up sp   Abiding
in God's Word causes it to become a living subs   e within

you. You see, you can have the Word in your mind, just taking up space, but that's not good. Abiding is not just repeating or reporting; it's a revelation. You can repeat or report what someone else has said about the Word, but you need to stay in the Word long enough yourself for it to become a revelation to *you*.

People need a revelation today. As I said, they are turning to everything else for answers. Tradition and religion have had us looking to everything else but to God, while what we really need is the Word of God.

We don't even have to feel anything to have a revelation from God's Word. Now don't misunderstand me. I like to feel the Lord and act all excited about the things of God as much as the next person, but I don't have to *feel* something to get excited about the Word. I know that God is not a man that He should lie (Num. 23:19). If God said it, He'll make it good if we'll believe Him properly.

I already told you how the enemy keeps a word from becoming a rhema to you. He steals it for one reason or another. And I told you that you will mess things up if you let the Word slip from you — if you don't keep going over it over and over again. Some people say they want a *new* word, a fresh word. Well, I would ask, "What have they been eating *lately*?"

What I'm saying is this: A person may like Italian food, but does he eat Italian food just once every five years? No, he likes it, and he's going to eat it as often as he can. Well, *spiritually*, why do we think we have to have some new scripture or new revelation, while, *naturally*, we eat the same kind of physical food day after day and week after week!

I know of a seasoned minister who takes the same Scripture text over and over again in a series of meetings he's been holding across the country. Many people travel to his meetings; I am one of those people. We know what text he's going to use before he ever says it. We can sit there and name his text! Before he even opens his Bible, we've already turned to the scripture. But nutrition comes out of it every time. That same Word benefits our lives — our families, our ministries, our businesses — every time.

So the important thing is not so much receiving a new word as *keeping the word fresh that we already have.* We do that by reverencing and respecting the Word and by keeping it before us, living and abiding in our spirits continually.

In each situation that we deal with in life, there is a rhema word to cover it! There's a word from God for you — even if you've heard that word a hundred times before. That word has enough power in it to cause miracles to transpire and situations to change in your life!

God's Word Cannot Fail, So Stand On It and Say, 'It Is Enough!'

That's why I know that when I have God's Word. God Himself is there. And I'm just going to "ride" that Word, because God's Word has not failed me in twenty-two years. The Word has *never* failed me!

God will always bring you out when you are trusting Him. He may not bring you out in the way you thought He would. If He did, then you'd be dealing in the sense realm. He will bring you out in His own way, but you have to get that Word abiding in you.

Did you know that the Word will not abide in you if you will not meditate on it? It will not abide in you if you don't stay with it, reading and meditating on the same verses over and over again. Your attitude should be, "Lord, I'm not going to leave this place until You talk to me."

I've had the Lord talk to me for a long time out of just one verse. I'd practically fall out of my chair. Sometimes I'd get up and run around the room because I was so excited. Then

I'd come back and sit in the same spot, and the Lord would begin talking to me again. So I'd run some more! I'd shout, spit, and holler!

That's why I like to have a hotel suite when I travel to minister. I've got to have some room! If I didn't, I'd tear the walls loose in that place! Sometimes my wife is with me, so I need a place where I can go and be by myself. Sometimes I'll be meditating in the Word in preparation for my message, and I get so excited, I holler out loud! I can't help it! It gets so good!

Victory belongs to us. It belongs to me, and it belongs to every person reading this book. I know it; God knows it; Jesus knows it; the Holy Ghost knows it; the Word knows it; and the devil knows it. And if you'll make sure that *you* know it, God, Jesus, the Holy Ghost, and the Word will bring it to pass for you!

Pay the Price to Take the Time

You need to spend time with the Word in order to know what belongs to you. Then, of course, your confession has a role to play. When you first start confessing something that the Word says belongs to you, do you know what is happening? You are confessing that Word to your spirit. You are getting that Word down into you. Then after a certain amount of confession, finally it becomes alive in your spirit, and the next time it comes out of your mouth, *production* will come. That Word that you have hidden in your heart will produce! That's the way the process works.

Sometimes when you're confessing the Word, it may seem like you're confessing for a long time. But there's a reason for that. When that Word finally becomes real to you, in your spirit, then when you speak it out the next time, the power and force of God will come out with it to cause whatever it is you're believing to come to pass.

Did you know that just because a certain scripture was real to you — in your spirit — at one time, that doesn't mean it will be real to you later on? It takes effort to *obtain* revelation from God's Word, and it takes effort to *keep* that revelation alive in you.

HEBREWS 2:1
1 **Therefore we ought to give the more earnest heed to the things which we have heard, lest at any time we should let them slip.**

Look again at that phrase "give the more earnest heed." In other words, that means *to pay close attention.* You need to value the things of the Spirit; cherish the things of God. Take hold of and appreciate the Word of God when you hear it. The most valuable, precious time of your life is when you are hearing the Word of God. Why? Because it extends your life, brings health, and resolves problems. So you need to value your time with the Lord and the times when you hear His Word preached. You don't want to be distracted when the Word of God is going forth. Satan will try to distract you, but resist him. In paying close attention to God's Word, there is great reward.

All It Takes Is One Word From God!

You could sit in church and listen to a man of God preach for a whole hour, but just one word from the Holy Ghost could be said through the preacher that could turn a situation in your life all the way around! There may be a situation in your life that you've been dealing with four or five years, but you could suddenly hear something taught from the Word of God that makes the difference. It's not so much what the *preacher* says; he is just giving you the Word. It's what the *Holy Ghost* does with that Word that you really need. The Holy Ghost will take the Word that the minister preaches and help you apply it to your particular situation.

The Holy Spirit will even tell you things the preacher *didn't* say. That's what the Spirit is there for — to bring forth the anointed, wonder-working power over a congregation so that the preached Word can become a living reality to them.

Some Christians just want the preacher to do everything for them. But no one else can pray and meditate on the Word for them. That's something they have to do for themselves.

Some Christians want *God* to do everything for them. But God is not going to do everything. They've got to play their part, and their part is to pay attention!

> **PROVERBS 4:20-22**
> **20 My son, ATTEND to my words; incline thine ear unto my sayings.**
> **21 Let them not depart from thine eyes; keep them in the midst of thine heart.**
> **22 For they are life unto those that find them, and health to all their flesh.**

You see, you've got to *attend* or *pay close attention* to God's words. You've got to spend time to incline your ear to His sayings. You've got to make the effort. Then this passage tells you the benefits that will come out of your doing these things. It all goes back to the power of the abiding Word. It takes work to get the Word to abide in you in power. But if you are hungry, you will do it!

If you are hungry to reap the benefits of the Word, you will pay the price to attend to His words and let them find lodgment down in your spirit. Jesus said, *"Blessed are they which do hunger and thirst after righteousness: for they shall be filled"* (Matt. 5:6).

That's why we are told in Hebrews 2:1, *". . . to give the more earnest heed to the things which we have heard, lest at any time we should let them slip."* Did that verse say, *". . .* lest at any time *God* should let them slip"? No, giving earnest heed and not letting the Word slip is something *we* are to do. If we let the Word slip, it will not be able to abide in us properly and produce the power that we need to overcome hindrances and to have abundant life. But when that Word becomes the sword of the Spirit, it cuts through adversities. It cuts through the natural and ushers in the realm of the *super*natural. Living by the living Word is a powerful lifestyle!

The Power of the Abiding Word In Your Prayer Life

My main text, John 15:7, is talking about your prayer life: *"If ye abide in me, and my words abide in you, ye shall ask what ye will, and it shall be done unto you."* Then looking at Ephesians 6:17, you will see that this verse is talking about your prayer life too. Right after Paul talks about the helmet of salvation and the sword of the Spirit, he says, *"Praying always...."*

> **EPHESIANS 6:17,18**
> 17 And take the helmet of salvation, and the sword of the Spirit, which is the word of God:
> 18 PRAYING ALWAYS with all prayer and supplication in the Spirit, and watching thereunto with all perseverance and supplication for all saints.

Actually, Paul is telling us to use the Word in our prayer life! You see, when a person is informed in the Word, has revelation from the Word, and is praying, he *knows that he knows that he knows* what belongs to him, and he is expecting to receive it!

One minister has said, "If you are praying without the Word, you are praying in the dark." So if you are praying *with* the Word, you are praying in the light!

The same thing is true about confession. If you are "confessing" with the Word, you are confessing in the light! The Bible says, *"The entrance of thy words giveth light..."* (Ps. 119:130).

So when you are praying or confessing in the light, you know that you receive what you are praying or confessing even before it materializes or before you actually have it in your hands.

You need the Word in your prayer life! You need a *rhema* word in your praying. So don't let the Word slip. What you have heard, put it to use and keep it available to you at all times, because you are going to need it again in life.

Have you ever thought about what it would be like not having the Word or not having Jesus? Oh, that would be a miserable existence! I wouldn't want to be in this world without Jesus and the Word. Every now and then, I think about that, and it causes me to appreciate what I have more and more. I'm so glad to be saved, filled with the Spirit, and living the life of Christ in the earth realm. It's a good life! I'm so glad that I'm alive and well and in the Word of God.

The Power of the Abiding Word Against Doubt, Discouragement, and Difficulty

You may be meditating and praying and just looking at different scriptures when, all of a sudden, a certain verse sort of leaps off the page of the Bible into your heart and then over to your mind, and it gets out all doubt! It cleanses your mind, and power comes upon you — an anointing — and you get up, dust yourself off, and say, "This is a done thing!" It doesn't matter what you're going through, you will count the answer a "done deal."

When you spend time with the Word, it becomes personal. You might receive a rhema word at church from the man of God because he's anointed, but you need more than that. You need personal fellowship and intimacy with God. In your car, in the bathroom, bedroom, or kitchen — wherever you are — you need intimate fellowship with God. You need to get alone with God. It's during those times that He will give you a trail of words for your situations. He will give you a rhema, a personal word. Then you will walk away from your prayer time and time of fellowship with the Lord, and you will know that you have things taken care of, because God revealed Himself to you.

That's why it's so important to learn to hear from God for yourself. Certainly, every now and then, a man who's anointed can lay his hands on you, and you will get free. You will get your answer, because it's the anointing that destroys the yoke. But the best way to get healing or whatever it is you need from God is to get it yourself.

Why do I say that? Because if the person who receives healing because a man of God laid hands on him doesn't get the revelation of God's Word for himself concerning healing, he won't be able to *keep* the healing he received when hands were laid on him. When he's at home alone, that sickness or those evil spirits will try to come back on him. They will try to manifest themselves, and if the person is not mature and doesn't know from the Word that healing belongs to him, he'll lose his healing.

As Christians, we have to finally grow up and learn how to lay hands on ourselves and let that anointing come out of our hands into our bodies!

It Is Finished!

A rhema word can cause you to walk in complete victory in life and in every situation and circumstance. It will have you and others confounded. A situation will seem impossible. Others will say it can't be done. But if you have a rhema word, then you won't even understand the words "can't be done." You won't even really hear it when others tell you something can't be done. It does not compute with you, because a rhema is pointed in one direction only. In other words, when you get a rhema, it is finished. Whatever your situation — that thing is taken care of!

Let me show you an example of how you can use a rhema in the face of circumstances and know that you've got the victory even though things still look bad. The example is the account of Jesus on the Cross of Calvary. He knew He was going to the grave, but He had a rhema word from God.

Jesus was bleeding up there on the Cross, saying, "It is finished!" (John 19:30). Well, what do you think Jesus meant when He said, "It is finished"? Some people think He was just talking about His dying on the Cross. But He was talking about something that hadn't even happened yet! He was talking ahead of time about what He knew was going to transpire.

You see, the act of redemption and our victory over sin, death, and the devil wasn't finished until Jesus died, was buried, took the keys of hell from Satan, rose again, and ascended to the mercy seat in Heaven with His own blood to make atonement for our sins.

So, you see, it wasn't actually *finished* up there on the Cross, yet Jesus said, "It is finished." Why did He say that? Because He had "inside information." He knew that His death on the Cross for the sins of the world was the route to the consummation of redemption. In other words, Jesus knew ahead of time what was going to happen, and He spoke it out, saying, "It is finished!"

In your own life, when you are attacked in some way and you're in some kind of a situation that you need to be delivered from, you can put God's Word on it — a rhema word — and you can say with confidence, "It is finished!"

You might say, "Well, I'm having a problem with my teenage daughter; she's not acting right." But if you will just get ahold of the abiding Word, you can look at the circumstance, even in the face of turmoil, and tell that circumstance, "It is finished!" That means you know that the situation is taken care of! Then you can tell the rest of the family after your prayer meeting, "It is finished." You're not anxious about it anymore, and you won't worry about it again.

I've been there when my back was against the wall, so to speak, and God has seen me through by depositing a rhema word in my spirit as I sought Him. I've seen it in the lives of others too. I've dealt with certain people whose situations looked impossible. But with God, *all* things are possible! There's power in the abiding Word!

Chapter 2
There's Spirit and Life In the Word!

It is the SPIRIT THAT QUICKENETH [makes alive]; *the flesh profiteth nothing: the words that I speak unto you, they are spirit, and they are life.*

— John 6:63

For the law of THE SPIRIT OF LIFE in Christ Jesus hath made me free from the law of sin and death.

— Romans 8:2

It is the Spirit that quickeneth or makes alive. Actually, if you read Romans 8:2 in the light of John 6:63, you can see even more clearly that the law of *the Spirit of life* and the law of *sin and death* are two distinctly different things. Why? Because the Spirit *quickens* or *makes alive!* The flesh "profiteth nothing." That's why we are to be led by the Spirit of God and not the flesh — the Spirit who makes alive is the One who reveals the things of God to us, those "live" words from Heaven!

Look at the phrase in John 6:63 "*. . . the flesh profiteth nothing. . . .*" Many times when we're dealing with the Word, we're dealing in the flesh. In other words, we just memorize certain scriptures and make some great-sounding quotes or confessions. But it's just flesh talking, and it won't profit anything, because it's not really in our spirit.

I want you to read that verse again: *"It is the spirit that quickeneth; the flesh profiteth nothing: THE WORDS THAT I SPEAK unto YOU, THEY are spirit, and THEY are life."*

It's the words that Jesus speaks to *you* — not the whole Bible or your "pet" scriptures — that are Spirit and life. You see, in every given situation, you need a fresh rhema from God. Even though a certain scripture worked for you last time, you'd better make sure that God wants you to use it this time, because He might have another scripture for you to use this time. Why? Because God believes in growth, not stagnation.

In John 6:63, Jesus was saying, "Not until I speak them to you will My words become Spirit and life." Until the Word becomes personal and dear enough for you to abide in so God can speak to you, it will not produce Spirit and life for you.

Notice Jesus *didn't* just say, "The words that I speak are Spirit and life." No, He said, ". . . *the words that I speak UNTO YOU, THEY are spirit, and THEY are life.*" In other words, it's the words Jesus speaks unto *you*, not just the words He speaks, that are Spirit and life!

You might say, "Well, the *whole Bible* is God speaking to me." Yes, but God might not be speaking and quickening the whole Bible to you if you are not available to hear what He is speaking — if you are not applying yourself to meditate and to get His Word to abide in you.

You see, as you spend time with God and His Word and make yourself available, God will speak a word directly to your heart. That's a rhema word; that's a word that is Spirit and life to you. It is a word that makes you cry, "*Ohhhh — praise God!*" It is a word that brings light and life and hope to your situation.

Your Words Can Carry Power

We have our pet or favorite scriptures, and sometimes we can get a little complacent with the Word. We hear so many scriptures, especially in Charismatic circles, but we've still got to be on guard, on duty. In other words, we've still got to be loving, appreciating, and *receiving* the Word if we want it to abide within us and if we want to have the power on the inside of us to be able to speak out that Word and see results.

You *can* get to a place where your words will be like Jesus' words. That may seem sacrilegious, but what I'm saying is, you can get to a place where the devil will not hear *you* speaking; he will hear *Jesus* speaking! The Word coming out of your spirit will carry power as if Jesus Himself were speaking it. The abiding Word will give you a *voice*!

When you are abiding in the Word and receive a rhema, that rhema word will come forth out of your mouth as the sword of the Spirit. And the enemy does not want to deal with the sword of the Spirit, because he has been cut by that sword before!

When you speak the Word in the light, with revelation knowledge, the devil knows who is talking to him. He knows that it's Jesus talking! He knows what Jesus did to him when Jesus took those keys and robbed him of the victory (Rev. 1:18). The devil knows that he is no match for Jesus, and that's the way he will know that he is no match for *you* — when Jesus is living on the inside of you and becomes real to you through His Word. Then when you speak that Word out, Jesus will manifest Himself. He will manifest His power on your behalf.

That's why I talked about the power of the abiding Word — the importance of abiding in the Word and getting it to abide in you. You see, whether or not the Word abides in you is up to *you*. It's not up to the Lord. It's up to you whether or not you will spend time meditating and abiding in the Word of God.

*Un*anointed Words Produce No Results

Getting the Word to abide in you also has something to do with the church you attend. If you go to a dead, dry church where the preacher is unanointed, there will be no "drive" in the Word down in your spirit. You will go to sleep and be discouraged and disgusted.

It's so sad when someone gets behind a pulpit and tries to give a talk about the Word. The message has no anointing on it at all. It's just as flat as dry biscuits! You have to just love that person and pray for him or her. Some people "went," but they were not "sent"! They don't have any anointing.

You can tell when a person has an anointing on his or her life. When you're anointed by God, you don't have to be running and spitting when you're preaching, trying to prove something.

It's rough trying to sit under someone with no anointing. One man can talk the Word, and the power will come, and another man can scream, holler, and grab everything he can, but still nothing comes! The anointing makes the difference!

> **1 THESSALONIANS 1:5**
> **5 For our gospel came not unto you in word only, but also in power, and in the Holy Ghost, and in much assurance; as ye know what manner of men we were among you for your sake.**

In this verse, Paul is talking about the effect the Word of God can have on your life, but it won't have an effect if it doesn't come out of the "spout" right! When there's an anointing on a man or woman of God in a service, God's people can enjoy the Word and get ahold of victory in their situations.

Even though you're in the Word of God for yourself, you will constantly have situations you have to deal with. No matter who you are, where you're from, or how many times you've prayed, you've still got to be on your toes spiritually. That's why there need to be a consistency in your church attendance. The Bible says, *"Not forsaking the assembling of ourselves together, as the manner of some is; but exhorting one another: and so much the more, as ye see the day approaching"* (Heb. 10:25).

The Power of the Preached Word

Christians are the most powerful people on earth because they have the life of God living on the inside of them. But too many are weak, broke, and defeated. It's because they haven't been doing what they should have done with the Word.

I wouldn't say these things to hurt you. I want to help you, and I'm not afraid to tell the truth. That's why the Holy Ghost moves so powerfully in my meetings — because I'm not afraid to obey God. We need some more Jeremiahs and Ezekiels. We need more people who will say, "Hey, the Lord says you're going the wrong way!"

Some will say, "Well, this is the way I've been going all of my life." Well, they're going the wrong way if the Word of God is not producing Spirit and life in their lives! They need to turn around and go the right way! If they will, the glory and Presence of God will move on their behalf.

As I just teach the Word in my meetings, the power of God will often fall, and people's needs will get met. They can hardly sit in their seats — the anointing is so strong.

I remember once I was just simply teaching the Word in a meeting that was held in a basement. The power of God hit that place so strong that people began to fall out of their chairs onto the floor! Another time, I was in another city, and the power of God came in the room so strong that every time I raised my hand, a whole row of people would fall down under the power of God! (You know, not every church can accept those kinds of manifestations. But when you're preaching to a congregation that can yield to the power of God, get corrected, and still yield to the Spirit, that's when God's glory comes in like a flood.)

When God's children accept what He is saying through the man of God and will say, "All right, Father, I see that. I'm not looking at the preacher; I hear *You* talking to me, and I'm going to go with it," then God's power can come in. God always confirms His Word with signs following if we will cooperate properly with Him and His Word. Bodies can be healed, minds can be delivered, marriages can be straightened out, relationships can be mended, and financial problems can be resolved. How? Through the Spirit and life that's in the Word!

When God comes on the scene, the results are supernatural. I'm not talking about just having church; I'm talking about the way it was on the Day of Pentecost when the Word was exalted and the Holy Ghost fell upon the Church. The needs of the people were met, because *power* came on that day!

When God's Word is preached and lifted up in a service, the Holy Ghost can move, and everyone in the house can sense His Presence. Everyone *knows* he's been in God's Presence. He doesn't have to wonder about it. He's seen and experienced things of the Spirit that he's never experienced before. The Lord is just good like that when His Word is preached in power. He is a good God, and He loves us, not because of *our* goodness, but because of *His* goodness.

That's why pastors have regular church services and special meetings as well. Pastors bring in other ministers to give confirmation to what they have already said to you, the congregation. It wears good in your spirit if you know your pastor is not the only one saying it. But it is the anointing that destroys the yoke. The Bible says, ". . .[it's] *not by might, nor by power, but by my spirit, saith the Lord of hosts*" (Zech. 4:6).

When the anointing comes upon a speaker, it comes upon you too. You know when it shows up. After a service one time, I talked to a lady who was in the service, and she said, "Something was all in my feet when you were ministering!" Glory to God! I began teaching the Word of God, got overwhelmed with the Presence and power of God, and that lady got overwhelmed too!

I love the Word of God, and I love being in the Presence of God, feeling His tangible Presence and power. I might be "minding my own business" in a meeting, just teaching the Word of God when, all of a sudden, there He is — the Spirit of God. I love it! Money can't buy it. That's why we have to stay in the Word and attend church, so we can be at the spout when the glory comes out!

We know that a rhema is a direct word spoken from God to you. But that word can come through another individual too. Your pastor can speak a rhema to you. He could be talking to the whole congregation, but God will use something he says that's just for you. What you do with it after that is up to you.

There is something special about receiving a rhema, a direct word from God for your particular situation. You might get it at home as you're studying, meditating, and praying, just seeking the Lord. But you need to not forsake the "assembling of yourselves together" either. You need to be at the right place at the right time. And sometimes that right place and time is at church, listening to the right speaker or minister!

When you've studied the Word, prayed, and then you go to a service or meeting where there is an anointing on the speaker, it sort of drives into your spirit the Word that you've already read. It puts a little spunk or spark into what you've been reading on your own and helps you with it. That Word gets pushed down in you, and you shout, "I've got it now!"

That's what the anointing is for. It brings life into a dead situation. The anointing of God resurrects "dead" things — circumstances you're dealing with — and it brings those things back to life!

I tell you, the anointing that comes with a rhema word from God will add years to your life. It will work on you for good. But it can go the other way if you're not in a church where the Word is preached boldly, confidently, and in power.

It could *take away* years from your life. That's why it's so important where you go to church and who you fellowship with. You need to go to a church where you can get the Word, because there's Spirit and life in the Word of God.

Spirit and Life Are Produced By the Abiding Word, Not Mere Talk

Now look again at First Thessalonians 1:5: *"For our gospel came not unto you in WORD ONLY, but also in power, and in the Holy Ghost, and in much assurance; as ye know what manner of men we were among you for your sake."* What is Paul talking about when he says, "in word *only*"? He is talking about the Bible. He is saying, "Our Gospel came not unto you in the preaching of the Bible *only*, but also in *power. . . .*"

You see, this is a good witness or confirmation that the Word of God needs to be in your spirit. It needs to become power — Spirit and life — in your inner man. But it can't be Spirit and life until it is *spoken* to you — until it becomes a rhema word, a revelation and a reality to your spirit. *That* is when the Word becomes power to you.

Sometimes we don't realize how much power we have. We are the most powerful creatures on the face of the earth. We as Christians are the most powerful species that ever existed. The Bible said, *"Therefore if any man be in Christ, he is a new creature: old things are passed away; behold, all things are become new"* (2 Cor. 5:17). One translation says, "If any man be in Christ, he is a new species that never existed before"! I mean, with the life of God on the inside of us, we can speak God's creative language. We are God's representatives, God's ambassadors, down here on earth.

You need to remind yourself who you are and then watch your words. Don't just talk to be talking. Guard your words, because what you say is very important. You want to speak words of life, words of power, and words of victory.

Paul said, ". . . *our gospel came not unto you in word only, but also in power, and in the Holy Ghost, and in much assurance. . . .*" For the Word of God to have that much power and produce that much assurance in your life, it has to be anointed. It has to be a rhema to you.

God is constantly speaking to us through His Word. He wants His children to have His Word and to be blessed by it. That's why He sent His Word — so it could become Spirit and life to us.

Stay Focused on What God Is Saying to You

You know, a lot of times, we get *too many* scriptures when we're going through a test or trial. We want to get books with everyone else's confessions written in them! We try to read what everyone else has to say, and we are not focused. We are trying to say what Brother Hagin or Brother Copeland says. But when you've got a problem, you have to focus on what *God* is saying to *you*. Then you need to stay with that word until it becomes Spirit and life to your inner man.

When you face a particular situation, test, or trial, pray in tongues with your Bible open, and God will talk to you as you seek Him. That is one of the major ways God talks to you. So if you have a problem, just start praying in tongues and seeking the Lord. Get out your Bible and read over different pages. Then, all of a sudden, you'll find out — there it is! A certain verse will become a rhema to you, and you'll know you have your answer.

A 'Rhema Word' From God Is a Mighty Force Against Problems!

When you receive a rhema from God, you will know that there is no force, enemy, problem, opposition, situation, circumstance, stronghold, or mountain that can hold you back! That rhema is a sword that will cut mountains down! It will cut circumstances down! It will cut strongholds down! It will cut opposition down! In every way, form, and fashion, you will know that you are the victor, because the power of God will come upon you, and out of your mouth the Word will come like a two-edged sword! It will change the situation and bring victory!

Paul said that the Gospel didn't come to the Thessalonians in word only but in power. In other words, the Word was *effectual* in their lives. It *did* something for them. Jesus said, *"It is the spirit that quickeneth; the flesh profiteth nothing: the words that I speak unto you, they are spirit, and they are life"* (John 6:63). You see, even though the Word of God is Spirit and life and is anointed doesn't mean it's going to be Spirit and life and bring the anointing on the scene for you. No, that Word won't do you any good if it's not revelation in your spirit man. The only one who can understand the Word is your spirit man. The Word is spiritually discerned (1 Cor. 2:14).

You Can Be a Voice!

Now let me show you that Paul had a rhema word from God — a revelation of the Word of God in his spirit. I also want to show you what Paul did as a result of that rhema.

You see, having a rhema word causes you not to consider the situation you're dealing with. Once you have a rhema word, you won't pay the problem any mind anymore, because you know it is already defeated! Then you can encourage people around you, saying, "It's going to be all right." They might say, "How can you say that? Don't you see what is going on?" But you can say, "It's all right; I've heard from God."

We know that Jesus operated on the same system. He had the Word abiding in Him and knew how to speak that Word with a *voice*, not an *echo*. In other words, Jesus' words were with *power*. He wasn't just a "repeater" of the Word.

The Apostle Paul knew how to speak with a voice too. In the following verses, we see that Paul had a rhema that enabled him to speak the Word of God with the voice and the authority of Jesus!

> **ACTS 27:20-24**
> **20 And when neither sun nor stars in many days appeared, and no small tempest lay on us, all hope that we should be saved was then taken away.**
> **21 But after long abstinence Paul stood forth in the midst of them, and said, Sirs, ye should have hearkened unto me, and not have loosed from Crete, and to have gained this harm and loss.**
> **22 And now I exhort you to be of good cheer: for there shall be no loss of any man's life among you, but of the ship.**
> **23 For there stood by me this night the angel of God, whose I am, and whom I serve,**
> **24 SAYING, Fear not, Paul; thou must be brought before Caesar: and, lo, God hath given thee all them that sail with thee.**

Verse 20 says that all hope was lost that the people on that ship would be saved. The experts on the ship had given up. They were crying out for life. By spiritual perception, Paul had tried to warn them earlier not to even set sail. But they wouldn't believe him.

Verse 20 says, *"And when neither sun nor stars in many days appeared, and no small tempest lay on us, all hope that we should be saved was then taken away."* They needed a rhema! And when you're in a situation like that, you need a rhema too!

Well, Paul had a rhema, and that rhema enabled him to have a voice! It says, *"But after long abstinence Paul stood forth in the midst of them, and said, Sirs, ye should have hearkened unto me, and not have loosed from Crete, and to have gained this harm and loss.*[Now here is the voice] *And now I exhort you to be of good cheer: for there shall be no loss of any man's life among you, but of the ship"* (vv. 21,22).

Can you imagine a man standing up in a boat full of water in the middle of a dangerous storm and saying, "Be of good cheer"! But that is the way Christians should talk. When you have a voice, it doesn't matter how a situation looks or feels, because the Lord has spoken. You have a rhema word from Heaven. And when you have a rhema, you can move from the realm of just being an *echo* to being a *voice*!

Just in the natural, imagine what would happen if you were sick, broke, and had just gotten fired from your job. Your sister walks in the house and says, "Be of good cheer."

You might say, "Are you crazy! I'm broke; I'm sick. My family is messed up, and you're talking, 'Be of good cheer'? You're crazy! I ought to slap you!" But, you see, in the natural, you couldn't understand it. You couldn't understand "being of good cheer" when everything around you is messed up.

It doesn't matter what you are dealing with, if you will be of good cheer and deal with it according to the Word, you will make it. It doesn't matter how much water has gotten into your ship or how long you've been going in the wrong direction. And it doesn't matter who told you that you'd never make it. You can be of good cheer. You can make it, because of the anointing and the Word of God. There's Spirit and life in the Word!

You may say, "Yes, Reverend Thompson, but you don't know my problem. You don't know what I've been going through." I don't really need to know your problem. I know what God's Word says. It says, "Be of good cheer"! Stay with the Word of God till you get that voice. Then speak to the situation with that voice. Stop looking at it and start speaking to it! Be like Abraham in Romans chapter 4, who "considered not" his circumstances. He only considered the Word of God.

ROMANS 4:19
19 And being not weak in faith, he [Abraham] considered not his own body now dead, when he was about an hundred years old, neither yet the deadness of Sarah's womb.

Paul, too, "considered not" his circumstances when he was aboard that storm-tossed ship. He only considered what he'd heard. Notice what happened: "[Paul said]. . . *I exhort you to be of good cheer: for there shall be no loss of any man's life among you, but of the ship."*

In other words, Paul was saying, "Listen, y'all can't die, because you're with me, and I have a voice."

You know, that's why it's important to be established in a good local church. Certainly, I've had people in my church who've died prematurely. I'm not making any excuses, but, in almost every case, I could see the reason why they died early. I could see what the problem was. There is always a reason for a person's dying prematurely. God does not take him or her out of here.

One key to living a full life is, you've got to be mindful of what you do and say and how you act. You've got to keep that tongue under control. The Bible says an unruly tongue that speaks the wrong things can kill you (Prov. 18:21; 1 Peter 3:10).

So we know that Paul had a voice. He said, *"And now I exhort you to be of good cheer: for there shall be no loss of any man's life among you, but of the ship"* (Acts 27:22).

Why could Paul say such a thing? Why did he have so much confidence? The answer is in the following verse.

ACTS 27:23
23 **For there stood by me this night the angel of God, WHOSE I AM, and whom I serve.**

Paul was saying, "I belong to God!"

Do you belong to Him? Belonging to Him is one of the qualifications for having a voice. There is another qualification in the rest of that verse: ". . . *and WHOM I SERVE."* Are you serving Him?

Notice what God said to Paul. First, God called him by name: ". . . *Fear not, Paul. . ."* (v. 24). Then God told him, ". . .*thou must be brought before Caesar: and, lo, God hath given thee all them that sail with thee."*

Paul spoke those words out with the voice of Jesus. Those words were rhema to Paul, and when Paul spoke, he spoke with power and authority.

Paul said, *"Wherefore, sirs, be of good cheer: for I believe God, that it shall be even as it was told me"* (v. 25). Paul said, "Be of good cheer, folks, for I believe God that it shall be even as it was told me!"

My brother and sister, when you've got the voice of Jesus working in your life, you can speak even in a storm. When everything looks like it's going awry and off the wall, you can speak, and everything will be all right. Your whole household could be rocking and reeling, but all it takes is just one member of that family with the anointing to walk in and say to everyone else, "Okay, y'all, everything's going to be all right. I've heard from God."

You see, if you hear from God, the situation may still look the same, but God has spoken to you and has told you that it's going to be all right. The problem can get worse if it wants to, but it doesn't make any difference to you! You've heard from God! That is what is so sweet about being an informed Christian who's walking in the Word of God and in the Spirit.

Don't Try To Copy Someone Else's Experience

A lot of people miss their miracles, because they are trying to get their answer the way someone else they know received *his* answer. In other words, someone may have been delivered a particular way in a similar situation. But you can't "piggyback-ride" someone else's faith or experience.

By way of illustration, someone may say, "Well, Sue got her answer by doing such-and-such. She had the same problem with her husband that I have with mine. She slapped her husband, so that is what I'm going to do: I'm going to slap *my* husband!" But her husband might be a different kind of man than Sue's husband! (Besides that, God is not in the habit of telling wives *or* husbands to slap their spouses!)

You see, you can't handle every person the same way. That's why you can't just mimic someone else's experience. You can't mimic your way out of your problems! When you're mimicking, you don't have any anointing. You're just following after someone else like a robot would. No, you've got to go the *sure* way. If you've got a sure word from God and God has told you to do something, you will not fail. You will speak forth the Word of God with the voice of Jesus, and your life will change!

So whatever God tells *you* to do, do *that*, and you will be successful and blessed. But, listen, God has got to get past your mind. He may tell you to do something out of the ordinary. You can do what you want with it, but I tell you, people have missed a lot of blessings because God told them to do something, and they didn't do it. It seemed silly, so they reasoned that it wasn't of God, and they missed it.

God can't do something for you unless you are operating in faith, so He has to put you out on a limb, so to speak, and let you operate on exactly what He said, not on what you think is the right thing to do. Then you've got to trust Him and expect *Him* to change your circumstance. And He will do it. So, whatsoever He says unto *you* — not what He says to your neighbor — do it!

That is why the Word of God is so precious and rich. A thousand people could read one verse of Scripture, and the Lord could speak to them individually and answer all of their problems from just one scripture! There's Spirit and life in the Word!

Everyone has things he or she has to deal with in this life — problems and adversities. That's why we need faith. We need good preaching and teaching. We need to pray and be led by the Spirit. We need to experience joy unspeakable and full of glory (1 Peter 1:8) and the Spirit and life that are in the Word.

I tell you, you need to get happy sometimes and just "lose it." Do you know what I mean by that? I mean, you need to roll on the floor, do "flip-flops," run, shout, holler, or scream — and just enjoy God! You need to forget about everybody and everything and just focus on Him. Act like you don't have a problem in the world and just enjoy the Presence of God. If you'll consistently do that, when you go back to look for a problem you had, it will be gone!

We need to stay excited about the Word of God, even scriptures we've heard over and over again. Let me tell you a little something about that. I received a revelation from the Lord on that one time. He showed me that when you read or hear the Word of God in a service, even verses you've read or heard many times before, if you will give God glory and show your appreciation by simply raising your hands and thanking Him when He shows you something from the Word, it will open up your spirit so He can give you more revelation.

Even during praise and worship when the choir or singer is singing, if you will open up to God and show appreciation, more revelation will come to you. And if singers and song leaders will open up and show appreciation to God, a stronger anointing will come upon them to sing. Some people in a congregation just sit there like stones while everyone else is praising God. But the anointing can make even stiff people move!

Some people don't ever get happy. They say, "Well, that's just my makeup. That's just the way I am." But that's no makeup; they're just holding back on God! I don't care how stiff they are, when the Holy Ghost begins to move, stiffness leaves, and even the most "sedate" people will move!

How can a wind come and you not move? The wind blows everything. If a strong wind comes, everything moves.

Well, the wind of the Holy Ghost blows on the abiding, rhema Word of God. And when the wind of the Holy Ghost is on, I don't care what your educational background is or how much you own, your days of being starchy and stiff will be over!

Chapter 3
Releasing the Ability of God Into Your Life!

And take the helmet of salvation, and the sword of the Spirit, which is the word of God.

— Ephesians 6:17

Ephesians 6:17 is talking about putting on the armor of God, including the sword of the Spirit. The Apostle Paul talks about the Word of God as being the sword of the Spirit — but it's not automatic. In other words, although the sword of the Spirit is the Word of God, the *entire Bible* is not *automatically* the sword of the Spirit to *you*. Why? Because the whole Bible isn't rhema to you; the whole Bible isn't alive and abiding in your spirit or inner man.

In order for a certain verse or verses — whatever word you need — to become a rhema word to you, those verses have to become "live" or living words in your spirit. *Then* you can use them as a sword of the Spirit in your situation or circumstance.

You know, sometimes you can read the Bible, and it's just as dry as it can be. (If that has never happened to you, you haven't been reading your Bible.) Despite its seeming dryness, the Bible is still alive and full of power, and something goes into your spirit when you read it. But on those occasions when the Word seems dry, your spirit is not receiving the revelation of the Word necessary for it to become a rhema to *you*. The Word is simply not "rhema" to you at those times. In other words, you can't draw on the Word and pull it out of you to use it effectively like you could if you had "fire" burning in you — the revelation of the Word. Jeremiah described it as "fire shut up in my bones" (Jer. 20:9)!

During those times when the Word seems dry, maybe you aren't spending the time with the Word that you need to spend to cause it to come alive in your spirit and become a sword to use in the situation you are dealing with at the moment.

As I said before, you need to take the time to become intimately acquainted with the Word of God. And becoming acquainted with the Word is not a one-time deal. For example, even if a word was alive to you at one time, and you used it once, you could go back to it later and you'd still need to get that word "hooked up" in your spirit in order for it to be effective.

Have a Solid Revelation of the Word

Just memorizing or being familiar with a scripture will not cause that scripture to work for you. The power and the life of that scripture are released when you *say* it. On the other hand, you can't just say it because you know it in your *head*. No, you have to know it in your *heart*. You have to have the *spirit* of faith based on the *word* of faith to cause that word to be a living sword to your spirit man! When you "believe and, therefore, speak," according to Second Corinthians 4:13, you will able to "cut into" your situation and see whatever it is you need or desire come to pass in your life!

I like to say it like this: *It's like your words becoming Jesus' words.* When the Word is alive in your spirit, and the spoken word is coming out of your spirit and not just your mouth, it's like Jesus Himself speaking!

So, you see, you have to spend time with God in His word until God speaks His Word directly to you. Then instead of getting up from reading your Bible feeling it was dry, you'll get up and you'll have a revelation, a sword of the Spirit, that you can use to effect a change in your situations and circumstances.

That's what I mean when I say that the sword of the Spirit, which is the Word of God, is not automatic. The whole Bible is not the sword of the Spirit to you personally. Only the words that become real to you are the sword of the Spirit to you.

For example, you could turn to a certain text in your Bible right now and start putting some claims on it, but it wouldn't do you any good if it's not in your spirit. Before you can benefit from a certain word from God, that word has to become a solid revelation to you. It has to be so alive that it's as if God is saying to you, "Well, this is what is yours; you can have it now because I said so." Then you have to take ahold of that and repeat it in faith.

I didn't say you were supposed to "parakeet" the Word or just speak it out of your head. No, you have to have the revelation that something in the Word is rightfully yours. Then you can speak it forth and take or possess what belongs to you.

How To Activate Your Sword!

In the previous chapters, I talked in-depth about how to receive a rhema. Now we need to understand how to *activate* and *work* that rhema. Then you can go ahead and speak to some of those situations you've been waiting on to change, and they'll obey you.

Previously, I talked about John 15:7 and John 6:63 — about how those verses connect and what their relationship is to our subject of the abiding Word. According to John 6:63, the words that Jesus *speaks* to you are *Spirit and life* to you. Those words are the sword of the Spirit that you can use to cut into your problems or circumstances and bring total victory into your life.

That's predominantly what I'm going to talk about in this chapter — the sword of the Spirit and the abiding, rhema word spoken forth in power. We know that before the Word of God can become the sword of the Spirit to *you*, it has to be an *abiding* Word and a *spoken* Word. *Then* it produces in you the spirit of faith and the sword of the Spirit, which releases the ability of God into your life!

> **2 CORINTHIANS 4:13**
> **13 We having the same spirit of faith, according as it is written, I believed, and therefore have I spoken; we also believe, and therefore speak.**

When you know how to operate in the spirit of faith according to this verse, it will be a tremendous blessing to your life. If you are operating in the spirit of faith, there's no denial in any realm for you. In no situation or circumstance can you be denied when you are operating in faith according to the Word of God! Why? Because when you speak the Word out of your inner man, the ability of God is released in your life. God's ability is released in your situations and circumstances to produce *power*!

God Will Perform His Word!

It's a powerful thing when you have the weight of God's Word coming against whatever is coming against you! And "heavy, heavy, heavy" hangs over anything that tries to oppose you when you are standing on God's Word!

> **JEREMIAH 1:12**
> **12 Then said the Lord unto me** [Jeremiah], **Thou hast well seen: for I will hasten my word to perform it.**

That's the way the Lord watches His Word. He is watching it to perform it. "To perform it" means that when you put God's Word out properly, God goes with that Word, and whatever you send that Word to do, God will see that the Word is fulfilled. He will see to it that it happens!

LUKE 1:37
37 For with God nothing shall be impossible.

That verse is a powerful statement, isn't it? It's a very short verse, too, but it says a lot. Notice what Mary said after she heard this statement spoken. She said, "...*Behold the handmaid of the Lord; be it unto me according to thy word*...(v. 38).

Look again at verse 37, this time in the *Amplified Bible*: "For with God nothing is ever impossible, and *no word from God* shall be without power or impossible of fulfillment."

God's Word Cannot Fail

I like that! No word from God will ever be without power. *Not one* of God's words shall be without power! When the Word of God deposits the ability of God in your spirit, nothing can stop you. God's Word is a mighty moving force. It's a supernatural force. And when it is properly applied, anything that stands in its way will have to move!

Look at Luke 1:37 in the *Amplified* translation again.

LUKE 1:37
37 For with God nothing is EVER impossible, and no word from God shall be without power or impossible of fulfillment.

I want to ask you a question. How long is *"ever"*? That means that there is *never* anything impossible with God. It means "no word from God shall ever be without power or impossible of fulfillment." That's powerful! That's why we need a voice and not just an echo — so we can experience the reality of this in our lives.

Say that out loud: "Nothing with God is *ever* impossible! And no word from God shall be without power or impossible of fulfillment."

The *New International Version* of Jeremiah 1:12 says, "...You have seen correctly, for I am watching to see that my word is fulfilled" So we know that God is a fulfiller or performer of His Word!

> **LUKE 1:45**
> **45 And blessed is she that believed: for there shall be a PERFORMANCE [fulfillment] of those things which were told her from the Lord.**

In order to release the abiding Word and the ability of God into your life, you first have to see and understand that God watches over His Word to *perform* or *fulfill* it. You need to know that if you have that Word abiding and active on the inside of you, *God* is active on the inside of you, watching to make sure that His Word is fulfilled for you. So if you act on the Word, God will watch that Word to see that it comes to pass in whatever way you need it to come to pass. He is watching over your *situation*, because He is watching over His *Word!*

You need to know the power that you have on the inside of you when the Word is abiding in you! All of Heaven is moving on your side! And when you speak, *Heaven* comes out of you, and no circumstance or foe can stand up against that power!

> **1 KINGS 8:56**
> **56 Blessed be the Lord, that hath given rest unto his people Israel, according to all that he promised: there hath not failed one word of all his good promise, which he promised by the hand of Moses his servant.**

I like the first part of that verse: *"Blessed be the Lord, that hath given rest unto his people Israel, according to all that he promised. . . ."* You ought to mark that and underline it in your Bible. Then it says, *". . . there hath not failed one word of all his good promise, which he promised by the hand of Moses his servant."*

It didn't say, "There has not failed *six words . . . .*" No, it says, "There has not failed *one single word* of all of His good promises!"

Listen, friend, when you get the Word working in your life, here's what will happen: *"Blessed be the Lord, that hath given rest unto his people Israel, according to all that he promised: there hath not failed one word of all his good promise, which he promised by the hand of Moses his servant"* (1 Kings 8:56). That verse will happen for you! When you get the Word in your spirit and speak it forth properly, not one word will fail to accomplish or bring to pass the desired result — *not one word!*

You know, there are a lot of people who say words, but their words don't come to pass. But when God gives out a word to you, and you apply that word correctly, it will never fail to come to pass! Heaven will be at your doorstep.

> **EZEKIEL 12:25**
> **25 For I am the Lord: I will speak, and the word that I shall speak shall come to pass; it shall be no more prolonged: for in your days, O rebellious house, will I say the word, and will perform it, saith the Lord God.**

God said, "The word that I speak shall be no more prolonged. . . ." As long as you're in this earth realm, you're going to be dealing with something. But if you learn how to use the rhema of the Word and the sword of the Spirit, problems will never be able to stand up against you.

God's Word Can Bring Life or Demolish Strongholds!

Anything good that you desire to come into your life, the Word has the power to create for you. And if something in your life needs to be demolished, the Word of God can take care of that too. The Word is powerful in any way you need it to be! God said His Word is sharper than any two-edged sword (Heb. 4:12). You can cut down bondage or oppression with it, or you can build up and bring life into a situation with it.

You see, a knife can be used in more than one way. You can use a knife to cut meat and vegetables, but you can also use a knife to defend yourself with if you need to.

With the "knife" or sword of God's Word, you can cut back the enemy that tries to rob you of the goods that God has given to you. So, you see, the sword of the Spirit can curse *and* bless: It can curse or demolish your *circumstances*, and it can bless *you!*

There may be some things in your life that you need to curse, because those things are hindering you from bearing fruit for the Kingdom of God. Jesus proved that principle to us by His cursing the fig tree (Matt. 21:19; Mark 11:14). In other words, Jesus' attitude was, if that tree wasn't going to produce like it was supposed to, that tree was "outta' here!"

What are some examples of things we need to curse in our lives? We know we need to curse sickness and disease, poverty, lack of fellowship in our homes, or whatever is spiritually hindering us in any way. And through the Word of God, we have the ability to speak to those things in power. We can command things to stop existing that should not exist in our lives!

Let's read Luke 1:37 out of the *Amplified Bible* again: "For with God nothing is ever impossible, and no word from God shall be without power or impossible of fulfillment." I want you to get the revelation in you that nothing is impossible with God. In the first part of Luke 1:37, God says, "With Me, nothing is ever impossible." Then in the rest of the verse, God goes on to explain *why* nothing shall be impossible with Him: *Because none of God's words is void of power!*

God's Word Can Bring Absolute Victory!

I like that phrase "no word from God shall be without power." It's so absolute. Not one word from God shall be without power or impossible of fulfillment! In other words, when you have the powerful, abiding Word in you, there is no such thing as your letting the devil or anybody else tell you that the Word will not be fulfilled and that you can't have what God has promised. You *know* better!

ISAIAH 55:11
11 So shall my word be that goeth forth out of my mouth: it shall not return unto me void, but it shall accomplish that which I please, and it shall prosper in the thing whereto I sent it.

God is saying, "Whatever I send my Word out to do, it will do!" He not only said it was going to accomplish something, but He said that it would prosper too!

No Word of God is void of power, so all you need to release the ability of God in your life is a word from God on the situation you're dealing with. Now it can't be just a *read* word; it has to be a *spoken* word — a rhema — in your spirit. You have to stay with it long enough for God to implant in you what He wants to implant.

God's Word Is a Right-Now Word!

A rhema word is a "now" word. It's not a word that's just based on your knowledge of the Bible. No, it's a fresh word from God's Word in each situation of life. If the Word is fresh, then it's alive in your spirit. A "live" word or a word that is alive and living within you grows and rises up in you, out of your spirit man, like yeast rises in bread. As that Word rises, you become bolder and bolder and bolder. You become more and more confident. You have the ability to look your circumstance square in the face and laugh, because you know it can't stop you.

The abiding Word in your spirit is a well of life springing up on the inside of you. When that Word is released to your mind, your mind begins to change. You begin to renew your mind and to think like God thinks. You can even get to the place where the Word is abiding in you so richly that you begin not only to *think* like God, but you *talk* and *act* like God too! You begin to see your situation from God's point of view. You can't do that unless you have the abiding Word in you. If you get that Word abiding on the inside of you, you'll begin to talk just like Jesus talked. Within the confines of God's Word and will, you'll curse what you want to curse and bless what you want to bless.

Abiding in the Word will give your life the same results that Jesus had in His life on the earth!

Look at Isaiah 55:11 again: *"So shall my word be that goeth forth out of my mouth: it shall not return unto me void, but it shall accomplish that which I please, and it shall prosper in the thing whereto I sent it."* This verse gives us a good picture of the Word of God not being void of power, because God says that the Word He sends out can't be stopped! Also, look at the word "shall" in that verse: *"So SHALL my word be that goeth forth out of my mouth: it SHALL not return unto me void, but it SHALL accomplish that which I please, and it SHALL prosper in the thing whereto I sent it."*

Results Are Guaranteed!

"Shall" is one of the strongest words you can use. God says His Word *shall* not return unto Him void but that it *shall* accomplish that which He pleases. What does "accomplish" mean? It means God's Word will come back accompanied by results! God's Word always brings results when it is abiding properly. *Properly meditated upon, properly abiding, properly believed in, properly yielded to, and properly spoken and acted upon, the Word will always be accompanied by results!* It will always be accompanied by victory!

God's Word will never fail you if you use it properly. It will never leave you "undone." It will never leave you dissatisfied, unhealed, or without victory. That's where abiding comes in. If you don't abide in the Word, Satan "cometh immediately to steal" the Word (Mark 4:15), for he knows if he can steal the Word from you, he is stealing your ability in God!

Therefore, you have to spend time with God's Word, whether you feel like it or not. You have to make it a personal agenda in your life. When you spend time with God's Word, you are spending time with God, Jesus, and the Holy Spirit. You are spending time in the Kingdom of God. Therefore, when you get up from spending time in that Word, you leave, not as a natural man but as a "super man"! You have the supernatural ability of God residing on the inside of you, and that thing to which you speak will have to obey you now, because you're not talking as a natural man anymore!

You Can Have Commanding Power!

We know there is only one God, only one Elohim, but when you abide in the Word of God, you become like Him from the standpoint of possessing supernatural ability and authority. When you speak to your mountain, that mountain obeys you! It *has* to obey you, because you are full of the Word. You have commanding power like Jesus had when He walked on the earth.

That's what we are here for — to represent God on the earth. The Church is to represent Him to the world. We are to speak God's Word in power and get the same kind of results from the Word that Jesus got in His earthly ministry.

In Isaiah 55:11, God said, "So shall My Word *be* that goeth forth out of My mouth." I like that word "be" too! It's a strong word. "Be" means it exists whether you like it or not! In other words, God's not *guessing* about it. He's not saying, "It might or might not be." No, He says, "It *shall be*"!

The Word Can Affect Your Faith Life
And Your Spiritual Walk

I know from personal experience that it's amazing what the Word of God can do in a person's life when he spends time with it. Spending time with the Word cuts sin out of a person's life; he hates sin, because the Word is purifying him. Even if he messes up, he runs to First John 1:9. He wants to be cleansed and to remain abreast with God and in fellowship with Him. He doesn't want to go to the throne of grace in prayer strapped with a lot of "baggage." He doesn't want to go in with doubt and unbelief; he just wants to enter right into the benefits and dividends of fellowship with God. He says, "God, You told me I could come boldly. Here I am. I don't have any known sin in my life, and I just want to do what You want me to do."

Abiding in the Word enables you to enter into God's Presence boldly, and it releases God's power and ability in your life in *every* situation. That means that everything is covered. That means, whatever you deal with from this day forward, there is a word from God that you can abide in that will release the ability of God on your behalf.

I want to show you something from Luke 4:32 in the *Amplified Bible.*

LUKE 4:32
32 And they were amazed at His teaching, for His word was with AUTHORITY and ABILITY and WEIGHT and POWER.

This is what is going to happen to you as you begin to abide in the Word more and more and let the Word abide in you. When you start doing John 15:7, this is where your life is headed — you will begin experiencing the *authority, ability, weight,* and *power* of God!

You can come out of any situation or circumstance by abiding in the Word. You'll have the same results that Jesus had. He faced some of the same kind of opposition, obstacles, and hindrances that you face.

Jesus was so persecuted that He could have let Himself be killed almost immediately upon beginning His earthly ministry. But He fulfilled the will of God and ministered those three years to show us how to work the Word in the situations of life. He dealt as the Living Word with the Word and the power of the Holy Ghost. Jesus' life was a pattern or example of how a son of God should live among fallen humanity and experience victory in the dilemmas of life.

Authority, Ability, Weight, and Power

When you have a rhema word — you become able to release the authority, ability, weight, and power of God and to live an abundant, joyous, victorious life.

Astonishing things happen in people's lives — things that are hard for many to understand — when they have a rhema word and speak that word with power.

When you have a rhema word, it puts your life on another level. Sometimes, even your Christian brothers and sisters will not understand why you are so blessed and victorious in everything you do. Most Christians are not operating in the Word; they are operating superficially. In other words, they've heard a little Word, but what the preacher says is not doing them any good, because they are not abiding in that Word for themselves.

When you begin to operate in the earth realm with a rhema word, it brings astonishment. You become amazing to others! They're serving the same God. They've been baptized in the same kind of water, but your life seems to take off like a rocket. You say things, and they come to pass. A person who hasn't been abiding in the Word will say, "Man, what's happening?"

Sometimes, people who don't understand the power of the abiding Word will think you're into witchcraft or something because of the power that's in your life. They don't understand the *real* power, the power of God. So they think you've gotten hold of something else — some other kind of power. They think, *It couldn't be God's power, because I'm saved; I have God's power, and it's not working for me like it's working for him. We both go to the same church, so he couldn't be operating in God's power.*

The difference between the one who is experiencing God's power and the one who isn't is, one person is abiding, and the other is not.

The Abiding *Word* Brings Abiding *Authority*

When you abide in the Word, a certain type of authority begins to emanate in your life that you can't obtain anywhere else except through the Word. That Word produces authority that causes demons and circumstances to obey you. The abiding Word gives you a voice!

Jesus said, *"If ye abide in me, and my words abide in you, ye shall ask what ye will, and it shall be done unto you"* (John 15:7). You see, you can't really abide in Jesus without the Word abiding in you. Jesus is saying in effect, "When you abide in My Word — when My Word takes up residence in you — then you are able to take up residence in Me. You can remain in Me, and the same authority that I have becomes yours."

The reason Christians don't have the authority they should have is, they don't have the abiding Word on the inside of them. They have a *written* Word; they have what they heard someone else say; they even have a lot of scriptures that they like to quote. But they haven't made those scriptures *theirs personally.* Those Christians are still an echo; they're just repeaters of the Word.

Don't Neglect Meditation in the Word

You've got to make the Word yours before it will benefit you; you've got to make it personal. You've got to say, "It's mine! It's mine! It's mine! If nobody else gets it, it's mine. I heard the pastor preach the Word, and I'm taking hold of it. I'm going to wrestle with that Word and meditate on it until it becomes a word for *me*! Then there's going to be a fight between Heaven and hell, because when I come out of my study room where I've been meditating, I will come out with a sword of the Spirit!"

Joshua 1:8 and Psalm 1:1-3 explain how meditating on the Word can move you from the natural to the supernatural so you can experience the authority, ability, weight, and power that's in the Word.

> **JOSHUA 1:8**
> **8 This book of the law shall not depart out of thy mouth; but thou shalt meditate therein day and night, that thou mayest observe to do according to all that is written therein: for then thou shalt make thy way prosperous, and then thou shalt have good success.**

> **PSALM 1:1-3**
> **1 Blessed is the man that walketh not in the counsel of the ungodly, nor standeth in the way of sinners, nor sitteth in the seat of the scornful.**
> **2 But his delight is in the law of the Lord; and in his law doth he meditate day and night.**
> **3 And he shall be like a tree planted by the rivers of water, that bringeth forth his fruit in his season; his leaf also shall not wither; and whatsoever he doeth shall prosper.**

Meditating on the Word gives you enough time to quiet down so your inner ears, your spiritual ears, can hear what the Word is saying to you. Most of the time we hear the Word with our "outer ears." In other words, we hear the Word naturally just as sound coming through our ear gate.

But in order to hear God, you've got to hear the Word down in your spirit. You have a set of ears in your spirit, because you have an inner man. That's where meditation comes in. Meditation feeds the inner man, but, first, it stops all the noise and gets the workplace, the kitchen, and the kids off your mind so that it's just you and God.

A Divine Cooperation

One thing I am endeavoring to help you understand is that receiving from God is a two-way street. It's not all God, and it's not all you. You are a co-laborer with God. You have to cooperate with Him according to His Word so He will have something to work with. The way God works is through *faith*. Faith in what? Faith in His Word.

Now look at Second Corinthians 4:13 again.

> **2 CORINTHIANS 4:13**
> **13 We having the same spirit of faith, according as it is written, I believed, and therefore have I spoken; we also believe, and therefore speak.**

This statement, "I believed, and therefore have I spoken" is talking about a rhema word, a word you have meditated on until it became the spirit of faith and the sword of the Spirit in your life.

Everybody in the church doesn't have the spirit of faith. Just because people are born again and have faith does not mean they automatically have the spirit of faith. Most people never operate in the spirit of faith, because they do not take the time to mediate and abide in the Word.

You can't operate in the spirit of faith just by quoting scriptures. Now, certainly, God will help you wherever you are in your faith walk, because He loves you. Thank God for mercy and grace. But if you're going to be a "mover and a shaker" in the spirit world, you'll have to have the Word abiding in you. You're going to have to enter into the spirit of faith that believes and speaks and sees Heaven moving on your behalf!

Maybe you can understand better why you have perhaps confessed some things in the past, but they didn't come to pass. It's not just confession or saying words; it's spending time with God before you begin speaking. Just saying something is not going to make it come to pass. The devil has to know that you understand what you're saying and that you're abiding in the Word. If you aren't abiding, the devil is going to ignore you when you tell him to leave. To him, it would be as if you were quoting from some history book! The devil doesn't pay any attention to a history book. But he does pay attention to the sword of the Spirit. He pays attention to the Word spoken in faith, and he has to obey it!

In Second Corinthians 4:13, there is a secret to the power of the abiding Word and to releasing that power. It is found in this statement: "... *according as it is written....*"

After abiding in that which is written (and permitting that which is written to abide in you), it becomes revelation knowledge to you and food for your spirit. After you spend time with the Word, then you say, "I believe; therefore, I speak." When you believe, the Word becomes a sword of the Spirit, and when you speak, that sword cannot be denied!

Have Word Faith, Not 'Bird' Faith!

Let's face up to the fact that there are a lot of words we've just been quoting and repeating. But we can't "parakeet" power! You've got to *have* the power!

You know, I am a Word-pusher! I want people to get ahold of the truth and experience the power of the abiding Word for themselves. I'm not trying to impress anybody in my preaching and teaching. I just want to be used by God to bless the people of God. In myself, I'm not any big deal. But God's Word *is* a big deal! God's Word is awesome, powerful, and exciting, and I get excited just talking about it!

A Sword in Your Mouth!

I'm talking about how to have and use the spirit of faith and the sword of the Spirit. Second Corinthians 4:13 says, *"We having the same spirit of faith, according as it is written, I believed, and therefore have I spoken; we also believe, and therefore speak"* (2 Cor. 4:13). Having the spirit of faith is sort of an introduction to or a prerequisite to having the sword of the Spirit. In other words, you can't use that sword before you actually *believe*.

That's why you can't speak against a situation or circumstance before you actually believe the Word you're using in that particular situation. Sometimes you have to speak the Word to yourself until you believe it. *Then* you can use that Word to speak to your situation!

The abiding Word will produce the spirit of faith within you. So spend time with God and permit that Word to abide in you. Meditate in that Word and abide in Jesus. Finally, the spirit of faith will be produced in you.

Now don't misunderstand me. If you are born again, you already have the *measure* of faith (Rom. 12:3). But after you have the *measure* of faith, you need to catch the *spirit* of faith, and the only way you can do that is by meditating and abiding in the Word.

Let's look again at John 6:63: *"It is the spirit that quickeneth; the flesh profiteth nothing: the words that I speak unto you, they are spirit, and they are life."*

The words that Jesus speaks to you *that you allow to abide within you* — they are Spirit and life. They will become the spirit of faith within you. In other words, *abiding*, the words Jesus speaks become the spirit of faith.

Prerequisites for Mountain-Moving Faith

Look at three of my main texts together, and then meditate on this thought: The *abiding Word* produces the *spirit of faith*, and the spirit of faith releases the *sword of the Spirit* in your life.

> **JOHN 15:7**
> 7 If ye abide in me, and my words abide in you, ye shall ask what ye will, and it shall be done unto you.
>
> **2 CORINTHIANS 4:13**
> 13 We having the same spirit of faith, according as it is written, I believed, and therefore have I spoken; we also believe, and therefore speak.
>
> **EPHESIANS 6:17**
> 17 And take the helmet of salvation, and the sword of the Spirit, which is the word of God.

When you have the spirit of faith, that means you've got a rhema word in you because of the abiding Word. That Word has come alive on the inside of you. As I said, getting the spirit of faith in you takes some time and effort. You've got to stick with the Word and meditate and abide in it long enough to be confident and convinced!

For example, the spirit of faith will bring you healing when you're convinced that by Jesus' stripes you're healed — you're so convinced that even if every symptom is showing that you're sick, you are too far gone with the Word to be sick! You can't accept it. The spirit of faith within you says you're well, so instead of siding in with your sickness, you side in with the spirit of faith, because the spirit of faith is stronger in your life. It, not the sickness, is the dominant force in your life. You can say, "I have the spirit of faith, and the spirit of faith is in me. I am well!"

Now people who do not have the spirit of faith won't know what you're talking about. They might think you're in some kind of cult and that you're just using "mind over matter." They don't understand that you are just obeying the Bible! You are calling those things that be not as though they were (Rom. 4:17)! You can call those things, because you have the ability and power to do so through the abiding Word and the spirit of faith. When you call something, it must show up!

Remember, there's authority, ability, weight, and power in the abiding Word. Jesus was our Example on the earth. He had the power of the abiding Word within Him, because it says, ". . . *they were astonished at his doctrine: for his word was with power*" (Luke 4:32).

I said that the abiding Word produces the spirit of faith, and the spirit of faith becomes the sword of the Spirit. Well, the sword of the Spirit produces — makes manifest — the authority, ability, weight, and power of the Word of God!

HEBREWS 4:12
12 For the word of God is quick, and powerful, and sharper than any twoedged sword, piercing even to the dividing asunder of soul and spirit, and of the joints and marrow, and is a discerner of the thoughts and intents of the heart.

One amazing truth that you need to grasp in order to fully understand the power that's contained in the Word is this: *The Word of God is the only commodity that can separate spirit, soul, and body.*

HEBREWS 4:12 (Amplified)
12 For the word that God speaks is alive and full of power [making it active, operative, energizing, and effective]; it is sharper than any two-edged sword, penetrating to the dividing line of the breath of life (soul) and [the immortal] spirit, and of joints and marrow [of the deepest parts of our nature], exposing and sifting and analyzing and judging the very thoughts and purposes of the heart.

Goodness! The Word of God is alive!

You know, you could hold your Bible in your hand and wave it around, shouting, "It's alive! It's alive!" But that book itself is not a living thing. No, it's the holy Word of God within the book that is full of life. Yet the Word is still not automatically alive to you personally until you make it *yours.*

You know that you are a spirit; you have a soul; and you live in a body (1 Thess. 5:23). And your communication and fellowship with God is in your spirit man. If you don't know how to get in a position to hear from God in your spirit, your flesh will answer first and try to influence you. That's why I keep emphasizing the Word. The Word is the only thing that can divide soul, or flesh, and spirit. It's through abiding in the Word that you become sensitive to God in your spirit. You can hear Him when He talks to you. He talks to you in line with His Word, and when He speaks to you from the Word, that Word in your own heart and mouth is a powerful living force that cannot be stopped.

Notice Hebrews 4:12 says that the Word God speaks is alive and full of power. *The Word of God has the same miracle-working power that is in Christ, the Living Word!* So, actually, when the Word becomes a sword of the Spirit, it's not just a confession anymore. It actually becomes a word containing miracle-working power!

Too many believers have been confessing, confessing, confessing, and they think that's all there is to faith, but it's not. If they were in faith, they would be getting some kind of result from all their confessing.

Jesus fully meant what He said when He made this statement, ". . .*whosoever shall say unto this mountain, Be thou removed, and be thou cast into the sea; and shall not doubt in his heart, but shall believe that those things which he saith shall come to pass; he shall have whatsoever he saith*" (Mark 11:23).

Jesus was saying that when you talk to a mountain of sickness, a mountain of financial problems, a mountain of family problems, or other kinds of mountains that come into your life, those mountains should obey you immediately. But many get hung up in the confession mode with their one or two pet scriptures. Spiritually speaking, they think they are riding, but they're really only *hitch-hiking*!

You are a powerful person as a new creature in Christ. With the Word of God handled properly, you can make demands on life, and life must obey you.

The Sword's Twofold Purpose

As I said before, you *are* a spirit; you *possess* a soul; and you *live in* a body (1 Thess 5:23). When the Word of God is abiding in you and functioning in you properly, it works on you first before it works on your circumstances, "separating" your spirit, your soul, and your body and getting your spirit in a position where you can hear God without the influence of your soul and body.

Your soul and body make a lot of noise, and that distracts you from the real thing — from hearing God in your spirit. But when the Word of God gets in there, it separates your spirit long enough to hear what God is saying to you. And when your soul, body, and spirit "come back together," so to speak, your spirit is in authority!

The first thing the Word of God does before it gets to work on your problem is, it operates on *you*! There is a spiritual "operation" that takes place. When you abide in the Word, the spirit of faith comes upon you, and the Word becomes a sword of the Spirit, the first thing that happens after that is, a spiritual operation takes place on *you*, and your spirit, soul, and body are "separated" so that God can just talk to your spirit. He can put into your spirit what you need in order to be strong and have the authority, ability, weight, and power that you need.

After the Word works on your spirit, it works on your soul to renew your mind, and it works on your body; it makes your body line up! It brings the body under subjection to spiritual things. It puts your spirit in the position of "General." In other words, your spirit becomes the one in charge. When that soul tries to come up, talking that soulish stuff, the spirit says, "No, that's not what we are going to do."

The body says, "*This* is where we're going." But the spirit says, "No, we're not going by the flesh anymore today. All instruction from now on comes from me. *I'm* in power and authority here according to the Word of God."

You have God's ability, then, because your spirit is full of power. Your body has come in line and doesn't want to run on the world's wave anymore. Your mind is no longer conformed to the world; it is transformed, because you have allowed the Word to abide on the inside of you. So now, with spirit, soul, and body in cooperation, you're pulling everything in one direction toward Heaven! You're ready to use the sword of the Spirit on your situation.

When you use the sword of the Spirit against your circumstances, there's something about that confrontation that will change your life. You will never be the same again!

Alive — Then Powerful!

Let me show you something else about the sword of the Spirit and Hebrews 4:12: *"For the word of God is QUICK* [or living], *and POWERFUL, and sharper than any twoedged sword, piercing even to the dividing asunder of soul and spirit, and of the joints and marrow, and is a discerner of the thoughts and intents of the heart."*

The Lord showed me a chronological order in this verse concerning the spirit of faith. He showed me that the Word has to be alive before it can be powerful. It has to be alive *to* you and *in* you before it can produce power in your life.

You're not going to get any power out of the Word until that Word becomes a "John 6:63" — Spirit and life — in you. Remember, John 6:63 said, *". . .the words that I speak unto you, they are spirit, and they are life."* But that's not automatic. The words that Jesus speaks are divine words. They were recorded as men were divinely moved by the Holy Ghost. But your mind and your body aren't going to pay any attention to those words unless you get those words into your spirit.

The reason the Word of God is not powerful in a lot of people is, the Word has not become "quick" to them yet. The

Word is not alive to them; it is not living and abiding in them, so no power is produced. How does the Word become "quick" or alive in a person's life? By his abiding in it. Then, according to Hebrews 4:12, after it becomes *alive*, it becomes *powerful* in his life!

Don't Deal With a 'Dead' Word!

You know, you can get into trouble if you try to use the Word against the devil before the Word is really alive and powerful in you.

Years ago, two preachers I knew were trying to cast the devil out of a man, and, after they had messed things up, the man's wife called on me to help them.

Actually, demons had taken over a man; his mind was completely gone. His wife finally called me after she saw that the two preachers couldn't help her. This was back in my earlier days of ministry when I was still considered a rookie. But I knew some things from the Word, and I had studied books by Rev. Kenneth E. Hagin and other men of God. I knew the authority in the Name of Jesus. I knew that demons could not stand the blood of Jesus.

I also knew that you didn't talk with or try to discuss anything with demons and that I had to look the man straight in the eyes when I was dealing with those spirits. Those demons can't be able to see any fear in you if you are going to deal with them effectively. You have to use the spirit of faith and the sword of the Spirit when dealing with demons.

Then I also knew that in order to deal with this situation, my life had to be clean. If you have some "skeletons in your closet" — some unconfessed sin — then you'd better get out of the house and not try to help when demon power is involved. Don't even talk about casting out devils if you have "skeletons" or "unright" things in your life. If you're living wrong and hiding it from everyone else, those demons will know!

When I got to that couple's house, the man who had demons was slinging those two preachers all over the room. When I walked in that room, I looked straight into the man's eyes and said, "In the Name of Jesus, by the power of Jesus' blood, come out of him." And the man snapped out of it — his mind was restored! He said to me, "Leroy, when did you get here?"

You see, the man came back into his right mind and called me by my name. Before that, he didn't even know I was there. But he was calm afterward; the battle was over. And all of that happened because of the living power of the abiding Word.

Alive, Powerful, and Sharper Than Any Sword!

We learned from Hebrews 4:12 that, first, the Word must be *alive*. Then, second, it becomes *powerful*. Then, third, it becomes *sharper than a twoedged sword*. It becomes that sword of the Spirit that Paul talked about in Ephesians 6. This is the chronological order of Hebrews 4:12 that the Lord showed me.

EPHESIANS 6:17
17 . . . the sword of the Spirit, which is the word of God.

This is what happens when you allow the Word to abide within you. It becomes alive, powerful, and a sword of Spirit, sharper than any two-edged sword, that you can use to cut through and defeat the circumstances of life.

Let's look at Luke chapter 4 to see how Jesus used the sword of the Spirit — the living, powerful, and sharp Word of God — in His earthly ministry.

LUKE 4:1-4
1 And Jesus being full of the Holy Ghost returned from

> Jordan, and was led by the Spirit into the wilderness,
> 2 Being forty days tempted of the devil. And in those days
> he did eat nothing: and when they were ended, he
> afterward hungered.
> 3 And the devil said unto him, If thou be the Son of God,
> command this stone that it be made bread.
> 4 And Jesus ANSWERED him, SAYING, IT IS WRITTEN,
> That man shall not live by bread alone, but by every word of
> God.

Now note again Second Corinthians 4:13: *"We having the same spirit of faith, according as IT IS WRITTEN, I BELIEVED, and therefore HAVE I SPOKEN; we also BELIEVE, and therefore SPEAK."*

In Luke 4, Jesus was using the sword of the Spirit, and this passage shows us how to use it too. Jesus didn't simply say, "It is written." No, He was saying in essence, "I believe; therefore, I am speaking it forth: 'It is written'!"

Paul talked about this in Second Corinthians 4:13. In other words, this is not something that only Jesus could do. Paul said, *"WE having the SAME spirit of faith. . . ."* But we can't just speak. We have to *believe* something. We can't just be saying words. No, we have a greater part to play than that. We have to *abide*.

Now your ability to destroy the devil's works doesn't come from you; it comes from the anointing that's on the rhema Word of God. You need to thoroughly realize that, and the devil needs to know that you realize that and are convinced of it.

There's a time, my brother and sister, when you have to turn from what you *read* about what is written to what is *said* or *spoken* to you *personally* from what is written. The Word has to go from being just the *written* Word to being the *spoken* Word.

It was the spoken Word that Jesus used against the devil in Luke 4. Jesus said, *". . . Thou shalt not tempt the Lord thy God"* (Luke 4:12). Do you know what I heard in my spirit once as I was reading that verse? I heard Jesus as saying to the devil, "You are no match for Me. I've got the Word down in Me, and it's not second-hand information."

You Can't Do Battle
With Second-Hand Information

You see, "It is written" could be second-hand information. But "It is *said*" is *first*-hand information. "It is *said*" means "I know for myself — *personally!*"

When the Word of God becomes a rhema to you, it's no longer just, "It is written," it becomes, "It is *said*." It becomes *spoken*. You have the attitude, "I heard it for myself. Nobody else has to believe it — *I* believe it! I know all things work together for good for those who love God [Rom. 8:28]. You can't tell me anything different, devil. I've got that Word on the inside of me. I know Romans 8:31 says that if God be *for* me, who can be *against* me! I *know* that. You think you're going to come against me, devil? Let me speak a rhema to you! I know that if God is for me, devil, you can't be against me successfully. You can't stop me. I know the authority that I have. I know the ability that resides on the inside of me. I know the weight and power that's on the inside of me.

"No force and no foe can stand up against me, because I *know that I know that I know* that it is not just *written*, it has been *said* to me. I heard God say that I'm the head and not the tail. I heard God say that I'm the healed and not the sick. I heard God say that I'm the rich and not the poor. You can't take it out of me. It's in my inner man like blood running through my veins."

That's why Job went through so much and then stood up and said, "Look here, may I say something? I went through all this stuff, but one thing I know — my Redeemer liveth" (Job 19:25).

When a person knows something, you can't take it from him. And that's what *knowing* is; it's having revelation knowledge — a rhema word — in your spirit.

I'm telling you, saint, if you come against a life-or-death situation, it's all right to have somebody praying for you. But in those life-or-death situations, it's so sad when the only confidence a person has is in somebody else praying for him. It's sad when he doesn't have a rhema — when he doesn't know the Word personally for himself. He may be quoting scriptures right and left, "up one side and down the other," but he doesn't have a rhema. He doesn't have the Word abiding down in his spirit.

I know people who've quoted scripture after scripture in life-or-death situations, and yet they died. They pulled every lever and pushed every button they knew, but they didn't make it. Why? Because you can't get a rhema just when you need it — you've got to have it down on the inside of you *before* you need it. Then when the need arises, you can meet that need head-on with the spoken Word of God!

I remember it was discovered that a woman in my church had a tumor on her brain. I and another minister visited her in her hospital room. This girl had the Word on the inside of her. It wasn't just written; it was *spoken* to her. It was personal to her. I said to her, "The Lord sent me to see about you. They tell me you've got a tumor. We're going to get rid of that today."

She answered, "Yes. We're going to get rid of it." We spoke with confidence, just like we were chatting over coffee or a bowl of cereal! She said, "Lay your hands on me." I laid my hand on her head and prayed, and afterward, she said, "Now I'm going to have more X rays taken. If the doctors don't want to order them, I'll pay for them myself."

That very day, she had more X rays taken. Before, she'd had a hole in her cranium with a tumor sort of "dancing" around in the cranial cavity under that hole. When they looked at the new set of X rays, they found no hole and no tumor! That thing dissipated that very day!

There was another woman in my church who needed an operation, because she had some kind of problem with her heart. I visited her just before she went in for the operation. For the past eleven years, she'd been faithful to the Word of God. She had that Word down in her spirit. I said to her, "I know you and your husband have prayed and have all your bases covered. I just want to add a short prayer of agreement to your prayer."

She said, "Go right ahead and pray, Pastor. And I'll tell you, I'll be back out of that operating room safe. I'll be all right." And, sure enough, God saw her through, and she was back up on her feet, strong and well, in no time.

It's wonderful to pray with members of my congregation when they're going through certain things. I'm their pastor; that's what I'm there for. But it's even better to get to teach people how to fend for themselves when it comes to receiving from God when it counts — in those life-or-death situations. In other words, they can fight for themselves. They're not depending on a man to do anything for them. They're depending on God. But the reason they're able to do that is, they *know that they know*! They have a rhema word for their situation so they can release the ability of God into their lives!

Chapter 4
The Secret to Obtaining Revelation Knowledge

When the Lord first started dealing with me about teaching this message, one of the first things He told me to do was to ask those to whom I was teaching not to become "over-familiar" with certain scriptures to the point they could no longer learn anything from those verses. In other words, if you are over-familiar with certain scriptures, you can "shut off" before God can add anything to what you already know. He can't add to what you already know, because you know what you think you already know! But you don't know everything. *You don't know what you don't know!*

One of the biggest problems with teaching Christians the Word is their familiarity with Scripture. It seems that when some believers get familiar with a particular scripture, the Lord can't talk to them anymore from that scripture. Why? Because they've already "got it." They've got everything they need to get from that verse; they've "arrived" where that verse of Scripture is concerned.

You have to remember that the Word of God is "pregnant" with revelation. No matter what revelation you've received from a verse of Scripture, that is not all there is to that verse. God can say something else; He can give more light from that verse. We must be open even though we're hearing scriptures we have heard over and over again.

You have to stay open when you hear and read the Word of God, especially when you're dealing with verses you've heard many times before. If you don't stay open, then you don't give the Holy Spirit the opportunity to say something more to you, advancing you in that area with those particular scriptures.

Some of the scriptures I'm sharing in this book are very familiar scriptures to most people. But in order to get from them what I believe the Spirit of God wants you to get, you are going to have to "forget" all your smartness! You're going to have to put aside what you think you already know, or it could mess you up and hinder you from learning more. Actually, having a teachable attitude will help you always keep the Word of God fresh in your heart and mind so that you can continually receive revelation and victory from God.

So don't ever become complacent or over-familiar with the Word of God. When you hear a familiar verse spoken, don't have the attitude, *I don't want to hear that again. Why, I've known that scripture since I was a little child.* Don't do that, because God has certain ways of speaking to us, and many times He'll use the same scriptures we are familiar with. When He speaks to us through these scriptures, we may suddenly hear them a different way than we've ever heard them before.

God's Word is pregnant with revelation; you could never exhaust the riches of revelation from the Word. We could preach the same scripture over and over until Jesus comes, and we will never exhaust the revelation that's in that Word.

Also, you could have the Word, but if you really don't know what to do with it, it won't bring about the dividends in your life that God wants you to have. So don't cheat yourself by having an over-familiar attitude toward the Word. Let it be fresh to you every time you hear it.

In this book, I'm sharing fresh revelation knowledge from the Word of God. But you've got to stay open to the Holy Ghost, who reveals and unveils the Word to us and imparts to us revelation knowledge. You have to stay receptive and expectant in order to receive from Him.

We must depend on the Holy Ghost to teach us. If it were not for Him, we would fall flat on our face! We should depend on the Holy Ghost to reveal to our heart the road to victory through God's Word.

I know you've probably already heard everything I'm teaching. But Peter said, *"This second epistle, beloved, I now write unto you; in both which I stir up your pure minds by way of remembrance"* (2 Peter 3:1). You see, I'm stirring up your pure mind by way of remembrance, because I want you to see it. You can't see the stuff I'm teaching just in the natural. Revelation knowledge doesn't come on the surface. I've got to have you deep enough in the water so that you've "swum" enough to know how to get ahold of it!

Part of the secret of obtaining revelation knowledge lies in your reverence and respect for the Word. When the Word of God becomes precious and dear enough for you to spend time with and to abide in, you are well on your way to doing great things for God and receiving great things from God.

One way you receive revelation knowledge is through the preached Word. That's why I believe it's important that you show a certain respect for the minister who's delivering the Word to you. By doing this, your spirit is submitting to God, and you are saying, "God, I reverence You and I reverence your gift. I just humble myself. I want to hear from You."

You need to have your spirit open to hear what God is saying to you. If you do, you can go from one level to another in spiritual things. If you do not, you will stay right where you are spiritually. Actually, you will probably go backward, because there's no such thing as just standing still or neutral spiritually; you're either going forward or backward all the time, constantly.

Getting 'Book of Acts' Results!

Because we are born again and in the family of God, and because the Spirit of God abides on the inside of us, we have the same opportunity to experience God's power as the believers had in the Book of Acts. I think the Book of Acts should come alive and be a reality in the Church today. It should come alive in individual believers, not just pastors, teachers, apostles, evangelists, and prophets.

The things that happened in the Book of Acts should be happening today in the lives of those who are walking with God and love Him. Believers today should have the ability to speak the Word of God and see the Word create what needs to be created; develop what needs to be developed; stop what needs to be stopped; curse what needs to be cursed; and bring into manifestation what needs to be brought into manifestation!

There might be some things you've been speaking to that are not obeying you like they're supposed to. You can make them obey you, but you've got to take it step by step. First, you've got to get some revelation knowledge from the Word and get to know Jesus the Living Word.

It's Not *Confession* as Much As It Is a *Relationship*

The secret to walking with God the way Jesus walked is revelation knowledge of the Word! Jesus had revelation knowledge of His Father. Jesus didn't have just a confession; He had a *relationship*.

I'm going to show you the secret to obtaining revelation knowledge from God's Word and living in continual victory in life. If you will start putting into practice what I show you, there will come a time when you are opposed by some circumstance that you will speak to it, and it will instantly obey you! I said *instantly*, not after ninety-five confessions!

Get To Know the Living Word

John 15:7 is talking about more than just reading the Word. Jesus said, *"If ye abide in me. . . ."* Notice that before we even get to the Word, we're talking about fellowship with Jesus. Fellowshipping with Jesus is how you get to know Him personally. And the best way to fellowship with Jesus is with His Word. We need to understand that it is impossible to abide in Jesus without the Word, and it's impossible to abide in the Word without Jesus, because Jesus and the Word are synonymous. They are one.

That word "abide" in John 15:7 brings the connotation of your spending effort and time, seeking to know God better and with greater intimacy. "Abide" carries with it the idea of desiring a deeper fellowship and walk with God and experiencing a greater knowledge of Him.

Then notice Jesus said, *"IF ye abide in me, and my words abide in you, ye shall ask what ye will, and it shall be done unto you."* So we know that the promise of this verse is *conditional*. Then, second, it is *personal*. Abiding in the Word is something that you do individually. In other words, an entire church congregation is not going to be abiding in the Word just because they sing good songs together on Sunday morning. And they're not going to abide in the Word as a congregation just because the pastor preaches good sermons.

Even though you have your confessions and are getting blessed to a certain degree, if you are depending on just hearing good songs and good sermons instead of abiding in the Word for yourself, you will not experience the full power of the Word on your behalf.

Learn To Work the Word for Yourself

You see, no one can work the Word for you. As I said before, it's *personal* and it's *conditional*. Now if you are willing to meet the condition and get involved personally with the Word of God, things can change in your life. They did in mine!

Then once you are abiding in the Word for yourself, there is something about properly *releasing* the abiding Word that you need to know. Releasing the abiding Word releases the ability of God into your life!

When you learn how to work the Word properly, some things you talk to — *instantly*, those things will have to obey you!

Don't Become Complacent About Faith — Learn To Expect Results!

To a large degree, we have just come to accept a lot of things over the years. We know about confession and about "keeping the switch of faith turned on." And that's good; we must continue to act on what we've learned. But there's another side of the coin we need to pay attention to.

For example, when Jesus cursed the fig tree in Mark chapter 11, that tree obeyed Him instantly. We know that it did, not because we *see* that it obeyed Him, but because it says that the fig tree died *from the roots* (Mark 11:20). What does that mean? That means that death was not just *upon* that tree; it was *within* the tree. There was nothing superficial or fake about it. It was as if the power of God "drilled" into the tree and caused it to die from the inside out!

We often quote Mark 11:23, *"For verily I say unto you, That whosoever shall say unto this mountain, Be thou removed, and be thou cast into the sea; and shall not doubt in his heart, but shall believe that those things which he saith shall come to pass; he shall have whatsoever he saith."*

Then we add something else to it, such as, "Well, I'm just waiting in faith." Well, that's the truth in a sense. We do have to continue to stand in faith in spite of what we see or don't see. But we shouldn't always have to wait for every opposition, problem, mountain, tree, or obstacle that we face to be removed. Some of these things should obey us *today*! If that's not happening for us, we need to work on changing our position. We need to come up a little higher in our knowledge and our expectancy. Then we will begin to have the things we say *when* we say them!

This will change your prayer life and your confession. Your prayers will not be dead and dry, because as you get a revelation of what Jesus is saying in His Word and what I'm teaching in this book, you will be expecting answers when you start talking!

Another Dimension of 'Asking' in Prayer

John 15:7 says, *"If ye abide in me, and my words abide in you, ye shall ask what ye will, and it shall be done unto you."* Now in the literal Greek, the word "ask" means *to make a demand on that which is legally yours.* When you know something is legally yours, you can make a pretty good demand! Well, how do you know something is legally yours?

If you have ever been in a courtroom, you'd know that it takes convincing evidence before a case can be settled one way or the other. If you were being defended, for example, your lawyer would have to have enough proof or evidence of your innocence to convince a judge or jury that you are innocent. If your lawyer has enough evidence, he will speak with confidence. And with the information he possesses, he can exert a certain authority in that courtroom. With the power he speaks with, he can get that judge to rap the gavel in your favor and settle the case!

Actually, with the information the lawyer has, along with the witnesses who are declaring your innocence, your case is really won before the gavel is rapped.

Similarly, by your abiding in Jesus and letting His Words abide in you, your will becomes His will. His knowledge becomes your knowledge. Kingdom dynamics begin to flow through your being, and you know without a shadow of a doubt that what you are making demands on must obey you. You are not talking out of your own strength or confidence any longer. You have the anointing of God's Word. Your circumstance doesn't hear you talking anymore; it hears *Jesus* talking!

You see, you have a right to make a demand on what is yours, because you have the revelation knowledge that whatever you're demanding is right! Properly abiding in the Word, you can boldly say, "Healing is mine! Long life is mine! Joy is mine!"

But that comes by abiding in the Word. When you're abiding in the Word and the abiding Word is in you, you can speak with the boldness — with the authority, ability, weight, and power that Jesus had when He walked on the earth.

Jesus Taught Us How To Obtain Results!

Jesus stayed here for three years on *this* side of the Cross — on this side of His death, burial, and resurrection — to show us how to live. He wasn't trying to teach us how to make nice confessions for years and years and yet never see any results! No, He was trying to teach us how to live in total victory and power in every situation in life!

Real, Abiding Faith Never
Comes Up Empty-Handed

We talked about the sword of the Spirit and how to release the ability of God into your life. As you abide in the Word and it takes root in your spirit, mind, and total being, then the next time you speak that Word out, it's no longer second-hand information. It's no longer a saying, a formula, or a slogan. It's the real thing, a rhema sword of the Spirit, and it's sharper than any twoedged sword! It will produce what it's supposed to produce, because real faith never comes up empty-handed.

Have you ever thought about the confession that you've been holding fast to for so long? Have you ever thought about why that fig tree Jesus cursed starting withering the minute Jesus talked to it? Have you ever wondered why that wind ceased to blow when Jesus commanded it to be still (Mark 4:39)? Why did these things obey Jesus instantly, while we're always having to wait for our change to come? There is a reason.

I may sound bold, but I've got to teach the Word like the Lord told me to teach it. There is a reason why people aren't receiving from God like they should be receiving, and I'm going to expose that reason. Part of the reason is, they fail to take the time to get revelation knowledge — a rhema word — from God.

How To Be Patient and Purposeful

An important part of obtaining the revelation knowledge you need to get the job done is *patience*. In other words, when something comes against you or there's some kind of roadblock in your life, don't just start speaking a bunch of stuff. Don't speak to that problem until you speak to the Lord, and the Lord speaks to you! Get your Bible and go to praying in tongues. Get your notepad. Tell the Lord what the situation is and just talk with Him until He gives you a scripture for your dilemma. Then go after it with the word He gives you. The anointing will rise up in you, and when you speak to the problem, it will have to leave you!

Too many times, we just quote our pet scriptures that everyone speaks in Charismatic circles. One of those scriptures is, "My God shall supply all of my needs according to His riches in glory by Christ Jesus" (Phil. 4:19). But most people are still broke after they've confessed this scripture over and over — day in and day out, month after month and year after year.

Supplier or Liar?

Let me ask you something. Is God a supplier, or is He a liar? Of course, the answer is, God is a supplier. The Bible says God is not a man that He should lie (Num. 23:19). But if you don't have the revelation in your heart of God as the supplier, you will continue to live without your needs met.

You see, a lot of people try to quote that scripture, Philippians 4:19, but they don't realize that there are some conditions to that scripture. For example, if that verse is not really abiding in them, in their spirit, it will not produce the authority, ability, weight, and power that it should produce.

Also, if a person is not tithing and giving, then he is not obeying the Word, and he is disqualifying himself from receiving the blessings of the Word.

Christians can have all kinds of pet scriptures. They have a scripture for everything! But a pet scripture doesn't work unless the Holy Spirit breathes on it, and it is believed and acted on.

So don't just automatically go to the Word and pick out your pet scripture when you're facing a need. Sometimes God will tell you to stand on a certain scripture that you haven't even thought of. That's why we need to seek God's face when we're dealing with the situations of life. If it is a family problem, for example, we need not go to our favorite family scripture!

That's why we often wait so long for a change in our circumstances — because the scriptures we are using are not rhema. When we get a rhema, it will cut right to the point and go to dealing with the situation!

Very seldom in life is there an emergency situation in which you can't take the time to abide in and meditate on the Word until the Lord brings something up for you personally —

revelation knowledge from the Word for your circumstance. (Sometimes there *are* sudden life-or-death situations. That's why it's a good idea to be constantly meditating and abiding in the Word.)

The reason people are not getting the full results like they should be getting is, they jump on the problem too fast. They need to take time to pray about their situation and see what the Lord wants to say about it.

I know from experience that when the Lord gives you a scripture and you act on it, it's all over for your problem! You don't have to confess it over and over to get it to work for you.

You Cannot Release From Your Spirit What You Don't *Have* in Your Spirit

Don't misunderstand me. I believe in confession; confession is important. But I don't believe in confessing five or six months over a five-minute job! I believe in confessing and releasing the ability of the abiding Word! But you cannot release what you don't have. In order for a Word from God to really abide in you, you have to pray and spend time with the Word and obtain revelation knowledge from the Word.

Meditate in the Word until the Holy Spirit begins to speak to you, permeating your inner being with that Word. Then that Word will become the sword of the Spirit in your mouth, and that which does not exist, the Word will create! And that which hinders the Word, the Word will move! There's wonder-working power in the Word of God when you work it effectively and properly.

As I said before, you can't "parakeet" power! You can't say, "He sent His Word and healed me," just because you heard somebody else say it. Just repeating the Word is not going to work for you. The Word has to become a rhema before it can become the sword of the Spirit and work for you.

Take Your Place and Take Your Possessions!

Laziness is one of the reasons the Word is not real to many people. It's been said that there is a God-ward side and a man-ward side to the promises of God. But, traditionally, we have laid all the responsibility on God. We have said, "Well, if God wants me to have it, He'll just do it." We haven't taken our responsibility and done our part to receive from God the things we need.

Actually, God has done all that He is going to do for you. Someone might reply, "Hush your mouth!" But it's true. All your victory and blessings have already been paid for by the Lord Jesus Christ. That's why the Bible tells us, ". . .*ye are bought with a price: therefore glorify God in your body, and in your spirit, which are God's*" (1 Cor. 6:20).

Your healing, your financial prosperity, your happy family, your long life, your joy, your peace, your happiness — all of that has already been paid for. But you can't get those things to come to pass in your life by looking somewhere else. You've got to get them from the Word. The Word has to become your mirror. In other words, you have to see yourself in the Word. And the minute you do, that Word has become revelation knowledge to you. Then you must speak the Word out — you must speak out what you see — and it will come to pass in your life!

Too many Christians just want to run, jump, holler, spit, and get happy for the Lord! But they don't want to take the time they need to in order to work the Word. They don't want to dig for the "gold"; they just want to skim the surface and parakeet what the preacher says. But it's working the Word that will make the difference in your life.

Don't get me wrong. You can quote or speak the Word in your life even if you have not received a rhema word. I often quote the Scripture, but I also know that there is a deeper level to which I can go.

The 'Turbo' Power of a Rhema Word!

Having revelation knowledge or a rhema word in a particular situation is sort of like having a turbo engine starting to turn on the inside of you! That Word becomes a spiritual turbo engine inside you, and you become a powerhouse! You *know that you know that you know* what God has said, and you don't need your pastor, your deacon or elder, your friend, or your neighbor to agree with you in prayer about it! You don't need fifteen people holding your hand to help you get through it. You don't need to get on the telephone to call the prayer lines.

No, you've got that "turbo" on the inside of you. It's the power of the Word of God, and it's just you and the Lord. Then you deal with your problem with that power and experience the victory that you knew was yours all along.

There's nothing like experiencing the power of the abiding Word in your life. Until you get ahold of that and start walking in it, you won't enjoy your walk with God as you should. You will always have to have people agreeing with you in prayer. You'll have to wait till the next time the church door opens to get delivered.

If a believer can't get delivered in his own home, he is not spiritually mature; he's still got further to go yet. If he has to wait till some "big-time" preacher comes to town to lay hands on him before he can be healed, he is not where God wants him to be. That preacher might never come to his town! That young believer needs to grow and develop and mature in the things of God for himself.

Have You Made God's Word Yours?

When I personally make this statement, "The Lord is my Shepherd; I shall not want," it is a reality to me. I'm not just quoting Psalm 23:1. The Lord *is* my Shepherd, and I *shall not want*! I am speaking forth reality. I'm not just repeating what David said. I'm not repeating what I've heard my grandmother and preachers say. It's not second-hand information. The Shepherd that David was talking about is *my* Shepherd. That verse is real to *me*, Leroy Thompson. And I literally have no wants.

I'm not bragging on me. That's the type of lifestyle that God has in store for each of His children, but it has to be by their working the Word, not just standing in the prayer line, waiting for someone else to get it for them.

It's okay to have someone else lay hands on you or prophesy over you. But you can get to the place where you can prophesy to yourself in your own prayer closet and speak the Word just between you and God and see the answer come.

I know firsthand what I'm talking about. I have experienced that "turbo engine" of the Word turning on the inside of me, and, particularly in the area of finances, I can't even *think* defeat anymore! I can't even *think* broke anymore. I won't ever let the words, "I can't afford it" come out of my mouth.

Don't ever say "I can't afford it." What do you mean, saying crazy stuff like that! Your Father owns all the silver and gold and all the cattle on a thousand hills (Ps. 50:10)! The earth and the fullness thereof belong to Him!

So why should you sit down here on earth with a Bible in your hand and God's Spirit living on the inside of you and say, "I can't afford it"! The only reason Christians are saying that is, some old religious spirit or some old tradition is still staying with them. The only way to come out of that is to get cleaned with the Word. John 15:3 said, *"Now ye are clean through the word which I have spoken unto you."* That abiding Word in you can flush out all of that old tradition and religious way of thinking that doesn't line up with the Word of God.

You can get to the place where you'll say, "There's nothing I can't have, nothing I can't do, nowhere I can't go, nothing I can't be, because, you see, on the inside that Word is working in me!"

Become a Spiritual Giant

Start working that Word, and you'll become the spiritual giant that God called you to be. God said that we are more than conquerors (Rom. 8:37). He said, "If I am for you, who can be against you" (Rom. 8:31). He said that all things work together for good to those who love Him (Rom. 8:28).

God meant that! That is not just for us to *quote*; that's for us to *live*! A person is on dangerous ground who tries to come against a believer of this Word! It's dangerous ground, because angels are camping around him, and he knows that they are there (Ps. 91:11). It's not a *quote* to him; it's *real* to him — it's revelation knowledge.

You see, for the promises of God to work for you, you've got to get in faith about them. You have to have the revelation of the Word until it becomes Spirit and life to you. You can't say, "My angels are watching over me" while you're crying all the time!

No More 'Down' Days

Years ago, one woman who was mightily used of God, made a certain statement, and she was exactly right. She said, in effect, "If you are a believer walking with God, you should not go down in defeat for one split second."

You know it's obvious when someone has the Word in his spirit and when he is just speaking out of his head or intellect. Something is different about the person who has a rhema from God in his heart.

When God speaks a word to you, you *know that you know that you know*! You get that Word in your "knower" where it becomes a reality, a rhema, to you. It becomes revelation knowledge. It becomes so real to you that, even if you see something else to the contrary, you don't believe what you see. You don't really see the situation as it *appears*, because you've got your sights on the Word. You only see what God said and what you are saying. And your seeing and saying things that way will change your situation.

I'm talking about "calling those things that be not, as though they were" (Rom. 4:17). You can't do that by just quoting some scriptures that aren't real to you. You've got to have a rhema, a sword of the Spirit, to do that.

As I said, many people think they are speaking God's language or that they're using the sword of the Spirit just when they speak from the Bible. Well, to a certain degree, they are. But they *really* speak God's language when that Word becomes a revelation or a rhema to them.

God through His Word has given you the ability to speak His creative language by your abiding in that Word. When you are really operating and functioning that way, you can create things in your life that do not exist. You might have some problem, but you'll be walking along, meditating and feeding on the Word until you get it in you. Then you'll turn on your problem and face it. That problem thinks it's going to take another step toward you, but it can't, because there you stand with the sword of the Spirit. Then you go to cutting with that sword, changing things with your mouth.

This Word of God works! I know from personal experience. I mean this reverently, but to a certain degree, I have to be really mindful of what I say, because what I confess will show up on my driveway! So I have to be mindful, or those things will just start coming when I speak.

'Know-It-Alls' Learn Little and Have Less!

Some people are saying all kinds of things and never getting anything. But if they'd listen to what I'm teaching, things could be different for them. You know, you can't teach someone who thinks he knows everything. When I'm preaching to a congregation, I don't look at those who shut their Bibles and just sit there; I look straight at the ones who are receiving what I'm teaching. Some people think they know all there is to know about certain scriptures that are familiar to us, such as John 15:7, even though their lives are like hay. Do you know what I mean by that? I mean, their lives are dry and dusty, like hay!

The 'Proof of the Pudding' Is in the Profiting!

Many times, we're saying a lot of stuff, and we're in the flesh. But remember John 6:63 says that the flesh "profiteth nothing." It is the spirit that quickeneth or makes alive! We say a lot of things with good intentions, but we're still saying it out of our flesh, because we never let it get down into our spirit.

But once you get the Word as a rhema or revelation in your spirit, then when you speak, it will be as if God is speaking. Romans 8:11 says, *"But if the Spirit of him that raised up Jesus from the dead dwell in you, he that raised up Christ from the dead shall also quicken your mortal bodies by his Spirit that dwelleth in you."* The Holy Spirit dwells in your spirit. Well, when the Word is revelation to you, it is revelation *in your spirit.* So when you speak it out, you are speaking it out of your spirit, and it's as if God Himself is speaking.

A Life Explosion

As you meditate in the Scriptures according to Joshua 1:8 and Psalm 1:1, the word that God quickens to you will leap out of that Bible at you! And whatever your situation, the case is closed! You won't need ninety-five scriptures on your confession sheet. You'll know that you know that you have it. You'll go on about your business, because that Word has taken hold in your spirit, and an explosion of life takes place!

I love it when that happens to me. There's nothing like it when God quickens my spirit, and I know that my flesh, the devil, and circumstances can no longer control me. The anointing that's on the abiding Word turns me into a "superman"!

That's where a lot of people miss it. They are quoting the Word out of their heads — and they're just like Clark Kent from the old cartoon. If you'll remember, Clark Kent never did have any power. Those people who are just quoting the Word out of their heads never go into that booth, so to speak, where the Word of God would explode as revelation knowledge in their spirit so that they could come out of that booth as "Superman"!

Speaking the Word as a "Clark Kent" is speaking the Word out of your head, your flesh. You've got to go down a little deeper and get into the "super" part by the power of the Holy Ghost!

That's what happens to you when that Word gets to stirring in you. It become a rhema; it becomes supernatural in your spirit. Then when it comes out of your spirit, it is supernatural to your mind. Your mind is renewed. After that, when it gets on your tongue, it becomes a supernatural sword of the Spirit. And that to which you are speaking will have to obey you — just like circumstances obeyed Jesus.

There are some things in your life that God is going to turn around for you if you will get ahold of His Word in your spirit and let it abide in you. It takes some time. These things don't come overnight. But when it happens, you know it. Ten thousand devils can't take it from you!

Be Honest With God

Some people are just faking it when it comes to the blessings of God. They are not really happy at all. They have adversity in their hearts and in their homes. They laugh about it on the outside, but inside they're about ready to knock their spouse in the head! Their needs aren't met, and they are grouchy and fussy all the time. They talk about their problems to their brother, sister, or close friend, but they need to be talking to the Lord and letting Him change the situation. He will do it through His Word!

I have a real marriage. I've been married for twenty-five years, and for the past twenty-two years, I've been finding out how to hook up with the Lord and His Word. I'm nobody special, but I have a special God! And He has given me a special marriage, special children, and a special life. The Word is working in our lives. I raised my children on the Word from the cradle on up. My oldest son is twenty-one years old. My oldest daughter is nineteen. They're rooted in the Word. They never argue about going to church. There's never even any discussion about it. They rejoice about going to church!

I know it's not like that in some families. Some people do not want to go to church; they just go because they don't want to go to hell. They don't even like the pastor.

(You know, most people can't really like a man of God the way they'd *like* to like him, because as soon as they start to like him real well, there he goes to the pulpit on Sunday and gets on their case about something. But that's his job — to show people where they're wrong and to point the way to Jesus according to the Word. People love the man of God, but sometimes they can't *like* him. The people didn't like the prophet Jeremiah too much. The Lord once told me, "Everyone is not going to like you, but people will love you, because they know you are telling the truth." Their flesh tells them, "I don't like that!" But their spirit man down on the inside says, "That's what I need.")

A Rhema Word Will Always Deliver!

I have a blessed life, because I found out the secret of obtaining revelation knowledge through meditating and abiding in the Word. The Word of God has produced in me a boldness and a confidence. I know for certain that the quickened Word in my heart — that which has become revelation knowledge — is never empty or unproductive.

When you get a rhema word, it is not empty or unproductive. What I mean by that is, the rhema word will always deliver the package! The rhema word will always take care of the situation. Read Isaiah 55:11 again: *"So shall my word be that goeth forth out of my mouth: it shall not return unto me void, but it shall accomplish that which I please, and it shall prosper in the thing whereto I sent it."* What shall not return to God void? The Word that goeth forth out of His mouth!

You see, once you get a rhema — once that Word is spoken to you and is alive in your spirit — you can speak like God speaks! Devils, demons, and circumstances are no longer hearing *you*; they are hearing *God*! It's as though the words are coming out of His own mouth!

The rhema word comes out of your mouth as a sword of the Spirit, not just English words or words in whatever your native language is. That word goes forth in *power*, and it does not return to God void! The rhema word goes forth in Holy Ghost, creative, dynamic, Kingdom power. And it has the same impact that it has in Isaiah 55:11 when it "goeth forth" out of the mouth of God! It *shall not* return void!

Just think about the Word of God that you speak never coming back to you void. Certainly, God knows where you are spiritually, and if you are earnest and sincere, you can speak the Word enough, and God is finally going to get to you whatever you are speaking in line with His Word. He knows that you love Him, and He loves you, but He desires that you go ahead and get the Word *in* you. He wants you to get to the place where you speak to circumstances by the power of the abiding Word, and circumstances obey you instantly.

Now, you know for yourself that you have made some confessions that have come back empty, and maybe they have been coming back empty for years. This message can change your life right now. I may be teaching this hard, but sometimes I have to "hit" people right "square between the eyes" so I can make sure they get it.

That's the way I minister. I like to challenge people.

People get hot at me and say, "Who do you think you are, talking to me like that! *I've* got the Word too!" But, no, people need to hear from the preachers and teachers that God has set in the Body of Christ. There's something that God is trying to get over to people through the minister that they probably won't get any other way. That's why He put different gifts in the Body. It's not that people don't know the Word, but God wants to add to what they already have.

So I come right at people when I minister. Some people can't handle it. Not every church can handle my coming to minister to them. They say, "Pastor, don't let that preacher come here anymore." They can't handle me because when I minister, I "go to their house," so to speak, and get in their closets! I talk about the facades and fronts people have. They smile at church, but when they get home, they're sad. That needs to change. The power of God can change it for them.

God's Word is true; it's alive, and it'll work in your life. It'll make you bold and give you confidence and joy unspeakable and full of glory! That's the kind of God I serve. I'm not talking about a "Sunday" god; I'm talking about a God who will work and move on my behalf seven days a week! He moves through revelation knowledge and the power of His holy Word!

Chapter 5
How To Make Your Mouth Work
For *You*, Not Against *You!*

I've been talking about the importance of abiding in the Word of God and receiving a rhema so that when you speak, you will have something to say that will produce results in your life. Some people are speaking too soon, and they're speaking out of their head and not their heart. Others have the Word in them; they just need to learn how to activate that Word. They need to learn how to make their mouth work for them and not against them.

How To Live 'After the Spirit'
So You Can Use the Sword of the Spirit!

It would be good for you to read the entire chapter of Romans 8. There are some powerful promises in that passage, but right now I want to focus on one portion.

> **ROMANS 8:1**
> **1 There is therefore now NO CONDEMNATION to them which are in Christ Jesus, who walk not after the flesh, but AFTER THE SPIRIT.**

Notice that phrase "after the Spirit." You're not going to walk after the Spirit and experience the first part of that verse — no condemnation — unless you have the Word abiding in you. You see, the Word reveals how to walk. For example, Romans 8:14 says, *"For as many as are led by the Spirit of God, they are the sons of God."* Many talk about being led by the Spirit, but you can't be led by the Spirit without the Word. It's the Word *and* the Spirit.

The Word and the Spirit Connection

Some people put so much emphasis on the Spirit that they leave out living by the Word. They are out of balance, and many times you'll find that these people do not live clean, holy, and victorious lives.

You see, the Word will clean you up. You can't be whoremongering, adulterating, fornicating, stealing, and lying on your tax returns, and so forth, and think you are going to have any power. You can't have power with God and at the same time be talking about your neighbor and putting people down with the words of your mouth. Good water and bad water won't come out of the same fountain, so you can't use your tongue for two distinctly different things — to bless and to curse (*see* James 3:11). God is saying, "Make up your mind how you are going to use your tongue."

Choose How You Will Use
Your Tongue — To Bless or To Curse!

You see, to use the sword of the Spirit to cut down situations and circumstances, you have to put a watch over your mouth. The Bible says, *"Let no corrupt communication proceed out of your mouth, but that which is good to the use of edifying, that it may minister grace unto the hearers"* (Eph. 4:29). You use the sword of the Spirit with your tongue, with the words you speak. Therefore, you have to bring that tongue under control if you want to receive the blessings.

You can't talk about the pastor or other church members and then turn around and speak with an anointing over your situation. Some people will complain about the choir, the ushers, and other things in the church and then say, "Bless God, I've got the power; I've got the Word of God in my mouth!" No, they don't. They don't have anything but sin in their lives!

This is an aspect of confession and speaking the right things that many take lightly, but it is a problem that has caused many believers to lose out on the blessings of God.

Some people will argue, "But I don't talk about other people." Yes, but many who say that are sure good at entertaining the bad things *someone else* says to *them*. They may not say anything bad themselves, but they "egg it on," so to speak, by listening to it, and they love every minute of it!

Be a Voice for God!

I'm going share with you how to be a voice, not an echo. Many Christians are really just an echo. They're not really a voice for God, because when you "echo" for the devil and repeat bad things about others and use your tongue for that which is unholy, you can't be a voice for God. To be a voice for God, you have to have the Word abiding in you richly (Col. 3:16), and you have to believe what you say out of your mouth. You can't do that when you're speaking in line with God's Word one minute, and the next minute, you're speaking in line with the devil and his ways.

If you really want to be a voice for God, you need to consistently speak in line with God's Word and then believe what you say! You're not just echoing what you heard your brother or sister say; you know and believe it for yourself. Then when you speak it out, you believe it, God believes it, Jesus believes it, the Holy Ghost believes it, all the angels believe it, and the *devil* believes it! In other words, the devil believes that *you* believe what you're saying, and his days of dominating you are over!

Did you know that when the angels hear God's Word coming out of your mouth with conviction — as a sword of the Spirit — they hearken to that Word and begin to move on your behalf to assist you. When the angels hear someone speak God's Word, they say, "Lord, let me take off on behalf of this person." Then many times, the person will mess things up by speaking doubt and unbelief.

Those angels wear out "track shoes" skidding in their tracks, because they can be almost finished getting the job done for a person when he says something negative, and they have to stop in their tracks! The angel might say something like this: "I never can complete a job for him, because he always opens his mouth and says something *negative* before I can get done what he has said that's *positive*! I'd like to have another assignment, please. Give me somebody else to work with."

Set a Watch Over Your Mouth

Your angel might be saying the same thing! It all depends on what you're saying! It doesn't matter how much you love God or your pastor, this is a "stand-up" thing. You can't sit down on the job! You've got to stay on your toes, so to speak, and put a watch on your mouth. The psalmist David said, *"Set a watch, O Lord, before my mouth; keep the door of my lips"* (Ps. 141:3). (*See* also Ps. 39:1; Prov. 13:3; 21:23.)

You've got to be diligent in this area of setting a watch on your mouth, because it's so easy to slip into the habit of saying that which is wrong. Rev. Kenneth E. Hagin tells the story of the time years ago when he was talking to another minister, a denominational leader, and the minister was talking badly about some other minister who had missed it in a certain area. Well, Brother Hagin is a man of few words, so he just sat there listening; he didn't say much. Then later, the Lord corrected Brother Hagin: "Did you say such-and-such about Brother So-and-so?" Brother Hagin said, "Why Lord, I didn't say that; that other minister said that." The Lord answered, "Yes, but you agreed, and that's tantamount to your saying it."

Brother Hagin never repeated what that other minister had said. Someone did ask Brother Hagin later about what was said and asked him if he agreed with the other minister.

Brother Hagin said yes, in effect, and that's what the Lord was correcting him about. So Brother Hagin had to repent.

There's Godly Gain With Godly Pain

I realize the things I'm talking about may cause you a little pain. But if you want the blessings that I'm talking about, there's no way around it. This is going to cause your flesh some pain, because your flesh likes to hear gossip.

You see, you're going to have to get some things right if you haven't already taken care of them, and you're going to have to keep them right. It will take effort on your part to watch the words of your mouth. You're going to have to make some adjustments with your mouth and your tongue. You're going to have to let the Holy Ghost take control of your tongue. If you say something, and the Holy Ghost says, "That's wrong," you're going to have to be man or woman enough to admit you're wrong. (I tell you, if you have to repent of something enough, you'll stop saying some of the stuff you've been saying!)

I know I had to repent a whole lot when the Lord first starting dealing with me about the words of my mouth. I've had to say, "Lord, I repent; I'm sorry. Forgive me." Then He's told me to go and tell certain people that I'd made a mistake. (I don't like to have to go back and say, "I was wrong," so it didn't take me long to learn!) I've had to say to some of the men in my church and even to the entire congregation, "What I said before was wrong; I shouldn't have said it. God has forgiven me, and I'm asking you all to forgive me."

Some pastors say, "Oh, I would never do that; my church will think less of me if I have to tell them that I missed it." But, no, it makes you bigger in their sight, not smaller, because they see that you are a man of God enough to tell them you were going the wrong way. If they see that you are honest, they will turn around with you and follow you as you follow the Lord.

It's important for us to "put a watch" on our mouth. We want our mouth to work *for* us and not *against* us.

JOHN 15:7
7 If ye abide in me, and my words abide in you, ye shall ask what ye will, and it shall be done unto you.

This is a powerful verse. One reason is, it can help your mouth work *for* you in life. This is the verse that causes Mark 11:23 to come to pass: *"For verily I say unto you, That whosoever shall say unto this mountain, Be thou removed, and be thou cast into the sea; and shall not doubt in his heart, but shall believe that those things which he saith shall come to pass; he shall have whatsoever he saith."*

You need to write that down! John 15:7 is the verse that causes Mark 11:23 and 24, Matthew 8:17, First Peter 2:24, and so on, to come to pass and be manifested in your life!

You see, a lot of times, we go to verses from which we know can render what we need and begin to speak those verses. But there are criteria to be met in order for those verses to work for you properly.

We often speak Mark 11:23, and, certainly, we have the right to speak the Word and claim the benefits of the Word. But it's not automatic — it's not a given fact — that our circumstances or "mountains" are going to obey us just because we are speaking. No, we must first get in a position where we know and understand the authority, ability, weight, and power of Mark 11:23. Then, spoken out of our mouth, that scripture will bring results!

The reason that Mark 11:23 has not been fulfilled in a lot of people's lives is, they are trying to speak it without *getting ready* or *preparing* to speak it. The way they are to prepare is through abiding in God's Word and obtaining revelation knowledge.

John 15:7 says, *"If ye abide in me, and my words abide in you. . . ."* That's talking about anyone who will abide in

Christ and allow His words to abide in him. Anyone who does these things has the right to make a demand on what is legally his. Jesus Himself promised it: *". . .[then] ye shall ask what ye will, and it shall be done unto you."* As I already said, that word "ask" means you have the right to make a demand upon what is legally yours.

I gave the illustration of a lawyer fighting a legal case. In the natural, a lawyer has to have evidence in order to plead your case! Well, spiritually, you need evidence to deal with the devil. You can't deal with the devil with second-hand information or with what you've read out of someone's book. You have to get the revelation down in your inner man and speak it out of your mouth. Now you *could* get it out of a book, but you'd better make sure that you get it down in your spirit so you'll know what you're talking about when you come face-to-face with the evil one who is trying to hold some part of your legal rights from you.

The Word Is a Living 'Substance' That Produces Living Results!

In John 6:63, Jesus makes a statement to us: *"It is the spirit that quickeneth; the flesh profiteth nothing: the words that I speak unto you, they are spirit, and they are life."* Now the dynamics of this verse are found in the statement, "They are Spirit, and they are life."

You see, the Word is a living thing. And if you properly know how to use the Word, you can release the living force that is in the Word to affect the affairs of life and turn things around.

John 6:63 says, "The flesh profiteth nothing." We as Christians are Word-carriers. But there are a whole lot of "Word-carriers" in the flesh. In other words, they are trying to carry the Word in the flesh — by mental knowledge, by memorization or by saying it over and over again. Just saying something over and over is not really what the Bible is talking about when it says, *"Let us hold fast the profession of our faith without wavering. . .'* (Heb. 10:23). God wants us to stand steady and sturdy and strong with the Word that's abiding in our spirit. But just saying or mimicking the Word over and over is not the same thing.

Two Levels of Confession

However, the confession of God's Word can be very powerful in the life of the believer. But the first part of confession is for *you.* You see, the devil doesn't pay much attention to your confession when you first start quoting the Word, because at that point, you are only quoting it for yourself — to get it down on the inside of you. That's why you do have to repeat the Word over and over — to get it past your mind and down into your spirit. Once it gets in you and becomes a revelation to your spirit, the next time you speak it out, results *will* take place.

A lot of people don't get results because they speak for a certain period of time, but they stop speaking before the Word becomes revelation knowledge or a rhema. Or they might superficially run with the Word and *think* they have it down on the inside. But they are not ready in their spirit, and that Word never becomes a sword of the Spirit. They don't get the powerful results that God wants them to have. Then they become discouraged and tempted to quit "holding fast" before they even enter that arena of revelation knowledge.

You know, some people go their whole lifetime in the church, being exposed to the Word, yet the Word never becomes a living force in their mouths to cause things to happen immediately. Over a protracted period of time, they may learn how to keep the switch of faith turned on, and praise God for that; they will receive some results in life. But after a certain period of time of abiding in the Word and allowing the Word to abide in you, you should not always have to wait and keep on waiting for the answer.

You don't need to be holding that switch so long in every single situation! If you're operating in the Word properly, some things should happen for you *now* — when you speak them out with the sword of the Spirit of the abiding Word! You ought to be getting some instant answers sometimes.

You know, if you're sick, you want to be healed *now*. If you're in pain, you want to stop hurting *now*, not five or ten weeks from now! I believe that by training yourself to make your mouth work for you, you can get to that place of receiving instant or quick answers!

What Are You *Expecting*?

This matter of getting answers quickly has a lot to do with your level of expectancy. What are you expecting! In Full Gospel, Charismatic circles, we have been training people to wait and to stand fast and long. But if you read in the Book of Acts, many times, they did not wait very long at all. They spoke the Word, and that which they spoke came to pass!

So we, too, need to get to the other side of expecting things to happen the moment we pray. I'm not saying we should forget about keeping the switch of faith turned on, because sometimes we do have to wait. Sometimes the adversary puts up a confrontation, and it takes a while for us to build up the momentum of the power of God.

By our being in these earthly vessels, we speak the Word, but we're not all the way in the Spirit sometimes. Sometimes we have to get stirred up in our spirit. That is why it's good to have good songs and good song leaders in services. They stir up the people and help get them into the Presence of God. Then the people can really get into the Word that's preached and become anointed. And when they become anointed, yokes are destroyed. The Bible says, ". . . *the yoke shall be destroyed because of the anointing*" (Isa. 10:27).

I want to point out something about another one of our texts, Ephesians 6:17: *"And take the helmet of salvation, and the sword of the Spirit, which is the word of God."*

I want to look at the last half of this verse: *". . .and the sword of the Spirit, which is the word of God."* The Spirit of God did not leave what He was talking about to our own interpretation. He plainly said, *". . .the sword of the Spirit, which is the Word of God."* First, notice He says, "the sword of the *Spirit*," not the sword of the *flesh* or the sword of the *mind*.

Then the Holy Spirit tells us what the sword of the Spirit is: *". . .the sword of the Spirit, WHICH IS THE WORD OF GOD."*

Now we already learned that the whole Bible is not the sword of the Spirit to *you*. What God *speaks* to you as you read, study, pray, and meditate becomes a sword of the Spirit to you. In other words, what becomes *revelation* can become a *sword*.

On the road of life, have you ever had to deal personally with a literal mountain hindering you in some way? If you're like most people, the answer is probably no. Have you ever had a problem with a sycamine tree in your yard that you wanted to move? (I don't have any sycamine trees, but I have oak trees. I don't want them moved, because I strategically planted them. My flowers are strategically planted. They're not unwanted, so I don't want to dig any of them up!) Again, the answer is probably no.

In the verses that talk about moving mountains and sycamine trees (Matt. 21:21; Mark 11:23; Luke 17:6), Jesus was talking in terms of things that become mountains or hindrances to us in life — things that hinder us from getting from point A to point B. He wasn't referring to literal mountains or trees. He said, "Speak to that mountain, and it shall obey you." But notice He didn't say, "Speak to it for three weeks" or "Speak to it for three months" or "Speak to it for three years."

Some people have been confessing the same things off and on for so long, they don't even expect what they're saying to come to pass anymore. Sometimes they eventually even forget what it was they were confessing and believing for!

You see, that's why you've got to "hear" God say something to *you*. Then, before it can be effective, you've got to stick with it. You've got to "Joshua 1:8" it! You've got to "Psalm 1:3" it! You have to meditate that Word; you can't mimic it.

There's a lot of mimicking going on. Folks have heard Fred Price say it, Kenneth Hagin say it, Kenneth Copeland say it, so *they* started saying it. (That's good in itself if they go on from there and get the revelation in their spirit of what they're saying. But if they're just repeating what they heard without having that relationship and fellowship with Jesus for themselves, then they're just mimicking, and nothing will come of it. But they can get to the place where they have that relationship and that fellowship tied up so well that when they say something, it's as if the Father is saying it and Jesus is saying it.)

Your life can change beginning today if you'll take your time and get the Word of God down in your heart before you try to speak to Satan and circumstances.

How Jesus Worked the Word

Jesus Himself told you how He worked the Word.

> **JOHN 14:10**
> 10 Believest thou not that I am in the Father, and the Father in me? the words that I speak unto you I speak not of myself: but the Father that dwelleth in me, he doeth the works.

John 14:10 is a vivid illustration of how John 15:7 works. In John 14:10, it's as if Jesus is saying, "Look, here is how John 15:7 works. Here is how I work the Word: I don't say anything on My own. I don't speak My own words. I speak what the Father speaks to Me, so *I* don't have to bring it to pass. *He* does it. The power to bring those words to pass existed when My Father spoke to Me. At that moment, the power was already there to bring those words to pass. All I had to do was speak the abiding Word, and the Father did the work for Me. He brought those words to pass."

That agrees with what Jesus said in John 15:7: *"If ye abide in me, and my words abide in you, ye shall ask what ye will, and it shall be done unto you."* He is saying in John 15:7, "If My words abide in you, just make a demand. You don't have to make it work yourself. Just make a demand, and what is legally yours will come to pass."

The Bible says, "In the mouth of two or three witnesses, let every word be established" (Deut. 19:15; Matt. 18:16). Well, I'm going to give you two or three more scriptures concerning the teaching and example Jesus gave to us. Then I'll talk more about it in another chapter.

The first scripture is in John Chapter 8.

JOHN 8:28
28 Then said Jesus unto them, When ye have lifted up the Son of man, then shall ye know that I am he, and that I do nothing of myself; but as my Father hath taught me, I speak these things.

This is another verse that coincides with John 15:7. In other words, Jesus was saying in John 15:7, "When you are abiding in Me, I will speak to you and teach you some things, so that when you open your mouth, Satan will know and demons will know that they're dealing with a sword."

When you've heard the Father and Jesus speak through the Word, then when you open your mouth to speak, hell is going to turn from you. And the Holy Ghost, Jesus, God the Father, and all the holy angels will point in your direction and say, "Who is that talking!" Angels are going to be at your command, because angels hearken to the voice of the Lord thy God. When you begin to speak the Word of God with the voice of Jesus — in the authority and boldness that Jesus spoke it — the angels won't know any better; they'll just turn toward that Word. They are ready to go to battle!

Now look at a second verse in connection with John 15:7.

JOHN 8:38
38 I speak that which I have seen with my Father: and ye do that which ye have seen with your father.

Jesus said, "I speak what I've seen from My Father. You do what you've seen from *your* father, the devil." Jesus was talking about revelation knowledge. In other words, He was saying, "My Heavenly Father reveals things to me. They're not just words; He *shows* them to me in My spirit. So I speak them, and it's not up to Me to bring it to pass. My Father has to bring them to pass, because He showed them to Me."

Jesus didn't speak a word of His own. In every situation, He got a word from His Father. That's why Jesus' words were so powerful.

In order for *you* to do that, you're going to have to have a relationship and fellowship with God; your intimacy with the Father has to be intact. You have to love Jesus, not just in a crowd, but when you are by yourself. When you are in your house or car, say, "I love You, Jesus."

Sometimes when I'm in my car, I have to pull to the side of the road, because I'm fellowshipping with Jesus, and He gets to loving on me so much, I have to pull over — I just can't handle it! I turn the steering wheel loose, and I just holler! I mean, sometimes, you can't drive and love the Lord too! When you start loving on the Lord, worshipping Him and telling Him how much He's done for you and how much He wants to do for you, sometimes you'll get to the place where you can hardly stand it.

Just thinking of how much the Lord loves me and how good He is to me makes me shout. Some people never experience the Presence of God and the anointing that destroy yokes. Some have never experienced God putting His arms around them and telling them how much He cares for them and that they can't lose a single battle, because no weapon formed against them shall prosper.

God wants that for them, but there's a price to pay. When they pay that price of abiding in the Word of God, their fellowship with God will grow sweeter and God's Presence will become a greater reality. Scriptures will become more and more real to them. Instead of just quoting Isaiah 41:10 and Romans 8:31 and 33, they'll hear the Father saying, "Fear not my child; I am with thee. Be not dismayed. I am your God. I'll help you. I'll uphold you with the right hand of My righteousness. Who can touch you? If I am for you, who can be against you?"

Oh, friend, God is a lover. He wants to fellowship with us so He can love on us and make Himself real to us like never before. But we've got to pay the price to get to know Him through the abiding Word.

I told you I'd give you three scriptures regarding the teaching and example of Jesus. Let's look at the third one in John chapter 12.

> **JOHN 12:49**
> **49 For I have not spoken of myself; but the Father which sent me, he gave me a commandment [word], what I should say, and what I should speak.**

Jesus says here, "For I have not spoken of Myself, but the Father which sent me, He gave me a *word* — what I should say, and what I should speak." Doesn't that sound like John 15:7, *"If ye abide in me, and my words abide in you, ye shall ask what ye will, and it shall be done unto you"*?

You see, the word "commandment" in John 12:49 means *word*. So Jesus said that God gave Him a word — what He should say and *speak*. John 15:7 says, "If you abide in Me, and My words abide in you, *speak* what you will. . . ." In effect, Jesus was saying, "If you meet the conditions of abiding in Me and allowing My words to abide in you, put your mouth to work for you. Speak what you will, and it has to obey you."

Chapter 6
How To Press in and Get Your Miracle!

In this chapter, I'm just going to "prophesy" or declare to you what God gave me. It has to do with speaking the Word of God with the voice of Jesus. But there are some things that have to happen first before you can speak the Word of God in such a way that it's as if Jesus Himself were speaking it.

Just by way of review, the word "quicken" has to do with your spirit. "Rhema" deals with your receiving a word from God in your spirit. The Bible as the written Word is one aspect of this. But when God gives you a *spoken* word from the *written* Word, that's another aspect altogether! When the *written* Word becomes the *spoken* Word, and you speak forth that quickened, rhema word, then the God with whom all things are possible starts to move on your behalf!

> **MATTHEW 19:26**
> 26 ...Jesus beheld them, and said unto them, With men this is impossible; BUT WITH GOD ALL THINGS ARE POSSIBLE.

> **MARK 9:23**
> 23 Jesus said unto him, If thou canst believe, ALL THINGS ARE POSSIBLE TO HIM THAT BELIEVETH.

> **LUKE 1:37**
> 37 For WITH GOD NOTHING SHALL BE IMPOSSIBLE.

If you haven't done so already, you need to underline these powerful statements in your Bible. Then you need to make these statements to yourself as many times as you need to in order to get it as a revelation in your spirit: "But with God, all things are possible!"

111

In Every Situation, All Things
Are Possible With God

Remember that statement. When the storms of life are coming against you — when it seems like you have no natural way to get out of your situation — tell yourself, "But with God, all things are possible!"

Look at Mark 9:23: *"Jesus said unto him, If thou canst believe, ALL THINGS ARE POSSIBLE TO HIM THAT BELIEVETH."* This verse tells us how we can, in a sense, get in the same category or class as God. Let me say it like this: *This verse can put us in a position to receive from God that which is not possible to receive in the natural!*

A Miracle Verse

Mark 9:23 is a miracle verse if you have "ears to hear" and your spirit is open to receive it. You can't just look at that verse like you've looked at it so many times before. Many times, we are familiar with certain scriptures and, because we know them, we don't look at those scriptures correctly. But unless a scripture is rhema to you at the time you need it, that scripture will not profit you. It will not benefit you if it is not quickened to you. The enemy doesn't mind your quoting the Word. But he does mind your speaking the quickened, anointed Word of God with the voice of Jesus!

As I said, the entire Bible is not rhema to you all the time. Ephesians 6:17 says, *"And take the helmet of salvation, and the sword of the Spirit, which is the word of God."* Yet we know that the entire Bible is not the sword of the Spirit to you all the time. Only that which you meditate and abide in will become quickened to you. And only that which becomes quickened can become a sword of the Spirit.

Did you know that the same scripture that is quickened to you at one time may not be quickened to you the next time you are dealing with something?

That knowledge will be of great value to you during times when you need a miracle. Instead of nonchalantly enunciating or pronouncing scripture verses, you will find a scripture that goes down into your spirit and becomes a reality — a revelation at that particular time to bring the power of God on the scene to do for you what you need to have done.

No *Quickening* — No *Power*

If a scripture does not come alive in your spirit, it will not produce for you a supernatural manifestation of power that you need to bring deliverance or salvation to whatever it is you are dealing with. In other words, just quoting scriptures is not going to get miracles for you. Even pet scriptures you hear over and over again in church are not going to get miracles for you if those scriptures are not fresh and alive in your spirit. Certainly, it's important to hear scriptures, because it says, ". . . *faith cometh by hearing, and hearing by the word of God"* (Rom. 10:17).

But just hearing is not going to get miracles for you. No, you've got to hear and *keep on* hearing. You've got to meditate on the Word of God until that Word becomes a part of you. Then you've got to do something with what you've heard; you've got to act on your faith.

JOHN 6:63
63 It is the spirit that quickeneth; the flesh profiteth nothing: the words that I speak unto you, they are spirit, and they are life.

The first part of that verse says, *"It is the spirit that QUICKENETH. . . ."* That means, it is the spirit that *makes alive.* You see, you can have the Word, but you need the Spirit to make that Word alive to you at a given time when your back is against the wall and no natural means can set you free.

Not a Formula But a Reality

At a time like that, you need to hear from God, but you need to hear from God in your *spirit*, not just in your mind. You don't need a *formula*; you need a *reality*.

Also, you need a rhema from God *when* you need it! Do you understand that? You need revelation from God's Word that's fresh *at the time you're dealing with a particular situation or circumstance.*

In every situation, in every battle, we need fresh manna from Heaven. We need fresh revelation from God. We can't just go to our familiar passages. Those scriptures have to come to *us*!

Gather Fresh Manna

I talked about how to get a rhema from God. First, you have to understand that it's the Spirit that quickeneth. Then you have to stay with God's Word long enough for your spirit to get in tune with God — until God gets hold of your spirit, and your spirit gets hold of the Holy Spirit, and the revelation of a particular scripture takes hold of *you*! Then the scripture that the Holy Ghost gives to you, that's the scripture you need to stick with until your answer comes.

Listen, friend, if you want miracles in your life, your flesh can't help you. It is only the *Spirit* that quickens or makes alive. When you stay with a scripture long enough, reading and meditating it, then all of a sudden, that verse just sort of jumps off the page at you, and it looks like all of Heaven at that time flops on you like a mantle! That's the anointing! That's the Spirit that makes alive and destroys the yoke of bondage in your life. That's the thing that will bring your miracle to you.

Many times, the reason we aren't enjoying the quickening Spirit and the miracles is, we have a whole lot of scriptures, but they have not become rhema to us. As I said, Satan doesn't mind us quoting scriptures, as long as we don't meditate on them — as long as they don't become real to us. Satan wants to trick us into just quoting a bunch of scriptures. He doesn't care if we quote the whole Bible, as long as we don't get into the Bible and meditate until that Word is abiding deeply in us, in our spirits.

We need to get quickened, not just last week, but this week, too, and *whenever we need it.* You may have received a revelation from the Word last week. That's fine, but this is another week! This is another time. This may be another problem you're facing.

A Rhema Is Received Personally, Not by Association and Environment

You know by now that you have to stay with the Word until it becomes a rhema to you. You can't just *say* it's rhema to you. You can't just say, "Rhema, rhema, rhema." And you can't say, "I graduated from RHEMA Bible Training Center" (or any other Bible school) and expect any results! The devil will say to you, "I don't care where you're from!"

While I'm on that subject, I've traveled all over the world, and I've met people who've said to me, "Hi, I'm a RHEMA graduate." RHEMA is an excellent school, but I often tell people, "Instead of saying 'right off the bat' that you've come from RHEMA, let some *rhema* come out of *you!* Then folks will know you're a 'rhema person.'"

Now I understand that sometimes you do need to give your credentials, but don't get "flaky" about it! When a person meets you and says, "Hi, how are you doing?" don't say, "I graduated from RHEMA. My name is John Doe!" No, just give your name, be quiet, and if you've got any rhema in you, it will come out of you!

You need a rhema to confess! If you want miracles in your life, you're going to have to stay with God in prayer and praise, with your Bible open, until God gives you the verse

He wants to talk to you with. It's not just running off and quoting scriptures that you know and then "holding fast to your confession."

I asked you before if you'd ever read your Bible when it seemed dry as any other book. Everybody at one time or other has done that. At times like that, you can barely get through your devotions! You see, the Lord doesn't just come down on you by His Spirit every time you read your Bible! You don't get full of joy and start dancing around every time you read the Word. No, sometimes, things in your life just go wrong, and if you've got problems in your family, for example, you could read your Bible like you've done every other day, and it could just seem like any other book at that particular time.

Learn To Press in Until You Hit a 'Gusher'!

It's during times like that that you need to just stick with it. If the Bible is not saying anything to you, just hold it up before God in prayer and start praying in tongues. Then go back to the Word, pray some more, go back to the Word, and pray some more, until you hit what I call a "gusher." Do you understand that word "gusher"? When you hit a gusher, that means life springs up out of that Word, leaps off those pages and into your spirit. Then you stand up and say, "I've got the victory now!" That's when the Word becomes rhema to you; it becomes a revelation to you. Then you can have your miracle. But the Word has to speak first. Then you have to speak the Word that's spoken to you.

Following this pattern of staying with God long enough to get your answer will bring you into another realm in your faith. It will change you into a different person. You will start blasting things away with your confession and with the Name of Jesus. You'll start blasting obstacles and hindrances away when you say, "I plead the blood of Jesus!" Why? Because you've got that rhema in your heart. You don't need any six-point outline you heard some famous minister preach. You need a rhema!

A Shortcut to Miracles

Being open in your spirit to the Word until that Word speaks to you is a shortcut to receiving the things of God that many people labor for time and time again. Now sometimes I understand you have to hang in there for the long haul. You have to stay constant and maintain your confession of faith over a protracted period of time. But you can develop yourself to the point where you can say and mean it in your heart, "I'm going to get my miracle today!"

I was ministering in a large meeting once and had a word of knowledge that someone was being healed of a breathing disorder. One of my church members was at the meeting and was sitting next to a woman who had a breathing problem. He told me that as soon as I gave out that word, something came out of her throat and fell onto the floor! She said, "Well, this problem is over"! She had been suffering, but the word I spoke out became real to her, and she responded and was instantly made well!

Oral Roberts has said, "A miracle is either coming after you or is passing you by every day." Every morning when you wake up, you need to say, "Lord, I expect miracles to take place in my life today — miracles in my family, miracles in my body, miracles in my finances."

I expect miracles in my life and ministry. I expect miracles in my ministry every hour. When people show up at church on Sunday mornings, I often pray, "Lord, work miracles in their lives. Give them all a miracle."

You see, you have to *expect* miracles before they will start happening in your life. And you need a rhema! You need a word from God, spoken by God especially for you and your situation at a given time. When you understand and believe that, you are going to feed on the Word like you never have before, and the Word is going to come alive to you like it never has before.

Leave your pet scriptures alone. They might bring you a manifestation five months down the road. But if you need an answer *now*, dig into the Word for some *fresh* manna. Dig in and *keep* digging in until you get it. Get into the Word and start praying in tongues and seeking God. Walk around your room like a wild person! Get happy — just you and God!

I tell you, I don't just want a dry Bible, do you? I don't want my Bible to be just ink and paper to me. I want it to be alive to me, in my spirit. I want it to quicken me. If you don't want the Bible to quicken you and become Spirit and life to you, you might as well read some history book or a good novel. But, you see, the flesh "profiteth nothing" (John 6:63).

Now when you are receiving your quickening, you have your soul and your body to contend with at times. Your soul and body don't always want to take the time to abide in and meditate on the Word. Your soul will holler out, "Hurry up and just take that verse! Just use that scripture!" You understand, you can get some results from quoting your favorite scriptures. But the Word will not be doing what it should be doing in your life if you don't take the time to get quickened with a rhema word from Heaven.

Many Christians have spoken out scriptures, but they have not let the scriptures speak to *them*!

The word that God speaks when you need to hear from Heaven — that is the word that is going to put you over. That is the word that becomes Spirit and life, a rhema, that can fix your problem. And God has a rhema for all your situations and circumstances of life. Once you get hold of that rhema, you will fearlessly look at your problem and declare, "I know you're there; I know who you are. But you can't touch me!"

Changed Forever

When God speaks unto you in any given situation, your life will never be the same again! You will come away from that situation victorious. Then the next time the devil raises his head, you're going to know what to do. You're going to say, "I'm going to get a rhema. I'm not going to spout off my little pet confessions. I'm going to get into that Bible until God speaks to me and that Word comes alive to me. Then I'm going to do something. I'm not going to open my mouth and speak a bunch of junk. I'm going to let Someone else do the talking! I'm going to speak the Word of God with the voice of Jesus!"

Let Your Elder Brother
Do the Talking!

I have a natural illustration that will help you see what I mean by the statement I just made. I have five brothers. I've put on a few pounds since then, but years ago, I was real skinny. One night before I was saved, I went to what we called a "playhouse." Those "playhouses" were dance places.

All the girls liked me. When I'd walk into those playhouses, the girls would all look to see who I was going to dance with. I was slender and dressed nice, and I always drove my brothers' cars! So I swapped up every night and had a different car to drive!

One particular night, I walked into one of those dance halls, and a big old boy — a "heavyweight" (he was big and out of shape) decided he was tired of the girls paying attention to me. He walked up to me and hit me! I mean, he hit me hard! He knocked me down, and I slid across the floor of that dance hall!

Do you know what I did? I didn't hit him back. I got up, got in my car, and went home to get my big brother! Then my brother and I went back to that playhouse! We walked in, and I said to that big guy, "Hey! Come here! What do mean, hitting me like you did!"

Now that big fellow knew that my big brother was a boxer. My brother wasn't a professional boxer, but I don't know if he ever lost a fight! He was a street fighter. When I hollered at that big guy, my brother was standing right beside me. I said, "I want to talk to you outside!"

My brother pointed at that big guy and said, "Leroy said you hit him. You know, Leroy is my little brother. Now step outside."

They went outside, and my brother put a "whipping" on his tail like his mama never whipped him! (In Louisiana, we say, "*whupped*"! My brother really put a "whuppin'" on that boy!) I mean, he really let that boy have it!

Now here's the lesson. When the enemy, the devil, hits you, don't "swing back" at him right then. Just "dust yourself off," get your Bible, and consult with your Elder Brother — Jesus! Consult with Him till you get a rhema and your Elder Brother says, "Come on. I'm going with you now. Let's go back and take care of that situation."

Now when that big guy hit me, I could have jumped on him and immensely lost the fight! Instead, I acted like I was giving up. But I knew once I explained everything to my elder brother that he would understand that I didn't start the fight. And when I heard my elder brother say, "Let's go back down there," I knew that fellow who hit me was in big trouble. I rode along in that car, thinking, *That old boy doesn't know it, but he's got a whuppin' coming to him!*

That's the way you have to do the devil. When he hits you, go get your Bible. Get yourself a rhema from God. Then go back and say, "Hey, Mr. Devil! I want to talk with you. What did you say you were going to do to me? I've got my Elder Brother with me now!"

Friend, miracles belong to you. You were born into a miracle family, the family of God. God doesn't want you waiting any five, six, seven, eight, nine months at a time just to hear from Him. He *wants* you to get a rhema. And when you do, the devil's days of whuppin' you are going to be over! When the Word of God speaks to you, power becomes available for your situation!

I'm going to show you exactly what happens when you get a rhema — when the Word speaks to you and becomes Spirit and life. When you really understand this, you are going to "home plate," and the devil is going to be in trouble where you are concerned. I am tired of the Body of Christ confessing, confessing, confessing, and never getting anywhere — never getting any results. That's not God's will. The Body of Christ needs a rhema!

Say out loud: "Lord, I want my rhema! Quicken me, Lord, with Your Word!"

It is the Spirit that quickeneth or makes alive. What the Body of Christ has been doing is going to Satan with a dead word.

Resurrect Your Hopeless Situations!

John 6:63 says, *"It is the spirit that quickeneth; the flesh profiteth nothing: the words that I speak UNTO YOU, THEY are SPIRIT, and they are LIFE."* You need to underline those two words "unto you" and put the word "me" near the word "you." Or write it down somewhere: "The words that He speaks *unto me*, they are Spirit, and they are are life." That means those words are alive; they can quicken you and make you come alive spiritually. They are life to the situation you are dealing with. *Those words become the resurrection to your situation — they become your victory!*

Now, certainly, we know that the Word of God is alive, because Hebrews 4:12 says so: *"For the word of God is quick, and powerful, and sharper than any twoedged sword, piercing even to the dividing asunder of soul and spirit, and of the joints and marrow, and is a discerner of the thoughts and intents of the heart."* But you have to get that Word alive in *you*.

We know by now that just saying the Word is not going to make it happen. That's what's been happening; we've been saying it, but nothing has happened. Certainly, I believe you need to say the Word to yourself and quote the Word long enough to get it in you — to get it to become a living, rhema word in your spirit. But *then* you need to start making your confession over the particular situation or circumstance.

What am I saying? Speak the Word long enough for that Word to speak to *you* before you go trying to speak it to the enemy. If you just go spouting the Word to the enemy before it's really abiding in you, he's going to know that you don't know what you're talking about.

You can't *quote* the Word to the devil. You've got to *speak* the Word to the devil! In other words, when the Word becomes a revelation to you and you open your mouth to speak it out, the devil doesn't hear *you*. He hears *Jesus*, because revelation knowledge is coming out of your spirit toward the devil.

Press in to Receive Your 'Rhema'

With the rhema Word of God, you win every time, but it will take some effort on your part. Take that phone off the hook, lock those doors, and get before God and say, "God, I've got something I'm dealing with, and I need a rhema."

It's only the Spirit that quickeneth. Remember, the flesh profiteth nothing (John 6:63). Jesus said, ". . . *the words that I speak unto you, they are spirit, and they are life.*" Only those words that Jesus speaks to you personally are going to work for you. The words that I speak or some other preacher speaks won't work for you. Now Jesus might speak through what I say, but if it's just me speaking it to you, it won't work for you. If what I say is going to be of any benefit to you, it has to go down into your spirit. If it doesn't, then the words I speak are just the words of one person to another person.

Look at John 6:63 again.

JOHN 6:63
**63 It is the spirit that quickeneth; the flesh profiteth
nothing: the words that I speak unto you, they are spirit,
and they are life.**

According to John 6:63, if Jesus doesn't speak the words
to you, they *won't* become spirit or life. I'm not taking away
from the Bible by saying that. I'm taking away from just
quoting words!

Words that *Jesus* speaks to you — words that become
Spirit and life — will work for you; they will produce results
if you know what to do with them.

In other words, if I'm preaching to you, and the words I
speak are just me speaking words, they won't work for you.
Those words won't be Spirit and life, and they won't produce
anything for you. But if I'm preaching out of my spirit and
not just my mind, the words I speak will be anointed —
they'll have that heavenly perfume or aroma on them — and
those words could become Spirit and life to you.

But if I am preaching out of my spirit, the only way you'd
be able to receive the words I preach is to receive them in
your spirit. That's why the Bible says, "If any man has an
ear, let him hear what the Spirit is saying to the churches"
(*see* Revelation chapters 2 and 3). If the Word preached is
going to benefit you, it's going to have to go down in your
spirit and speak to you personally.

Some people think that just because they have their Bible
and are quoting a bunch of scriptures, they don't need a
pastor. They think they don't need an undershepherd. They
say, "I read and pray at my house." Well, that's good. They
should read and pray at their house. But the Bible they have
at home says, "Forsake not the assembling of yourselves
together" (Heb. 10:25).

If you're really saved, you ought to want to go to church
and other special meetings. You ought to want to go there
and see your brethren. Where you're weak, they may be

strong, and where they're weak, you may be strong. You need the fellowship of other believers.

You can always tell when people are too "spiritual" and have gotten off-track. They don't want to go to church; they don't want fellowship. Those people might have "revelations," all right. But they don't have any rhema or word from God — they just ate too much spaghetti!

'Cut' Your Way Through Obstacles And Receive Your Miracle!

When the Word of God becomes a rhema to you, a living reality — a revelation to you at some particular moment, for your situation — there's going to be some cutting going on! Some spiritual surgery will be about to take place. The devil had better get out of your way, because you'll become a surgeon with the sword of the Spirit.

Trouble may have come your way to defeat you. But with the rhema Word of God, you're going back to that situation anointed! You're going back to work on your case, but you're going with power! Why? Because you've got revelation knowledge in your spirit. You can tell the devil, "Get back from me. I've got victory! Victory is mine!"

The Lord gave me a visual illustration to show you how to make using the sword of the Spirit more real to you. The Bible says, *"He that believeth on me, as the scripture hath said, out of his belly shall flow rivers of living water"* (John 7:38).

Your "belly" in this verse is your spirit. So, just for your own faith, when you're dealing with something and you get that rhema, reach with your closed fist toward your belly or spirit and get out that sword! If you imagine that your spirit is the scabbard or holder where a sword is kept in the natural, just reach in there, get out your sword, and start cutting with it!

Doing that will help your faith. When you get a rhema in

your spirit, get up from your desk, prayer closet, or place where you were meditating, and reach into your spirit for that sword! Get ahold of that sword, that rhema, in your spirit. Then pull it out and declare war! With the sword of the Spirit, which is the rhema Word of God, the devil is no match for you in your situation. You are the devil's master; he must obey you!

Don't Let Go of God!

By now you know that it is possible to get hold of God and get His Word on your problem. You remember Jacob told God, "I'm not turning You loose till You bless me' (Gen. 32:26). The angel looked at his watch and said, "I've got to go now"! But Jacob looked at his watch and said, "Yes, but I'm not blessed yet. We are going to be here till daybreak, 'cause I'm not letting You go until You bless me!"

Well, that's what you've got to do. You have to be like a pit-bull dog! In other words, when you get on a trail of God's Word and finally get ahold of it, you have to lock into it and refuse to open your jaw! Just take it and don't turn it loose till you see the answer! And, you know, the Lord likes that. The Lord likes someone who will be bold and not give up. The Word says, *"Let us therefore come BOLDLY unto the throne of grace, that we may obtain mercy, and find grace to help in time of need"* (Heb. 4:16). It excites God when one of His children says, "God, You have to do this, because Your Word says so. And if You don't do it, I'm going to tell on You!"

Certainly, we are to be reverent before God. That's what it means to fear the Lord — to be reverent before Him. But, you know, some people are afraid of God. They are actually in the family of God, yet they are afraid. They think God is some big man sitting up on the throne who can't be talked to or communicated with. To them, He's not humorous; He's unhappy, and He wears a black suit all the time!

But, no! That's not the God I serve! I can talk to my God.

I can go boldly to His throne of grace for mercy and grace to help me in my time of need (Heb. 4:16)! I can say, "God, I've got to get out of this situation, and I'm not going to leave Your Presence till we get out of it. If I'm in it, You're in it, because I'm wearing Your Name."

God loves it when you go to Him and say from your heart, "God, I want what is rightfully mine. The devil says I can't have it, but I know I can, and I stopped by to get it! I'm not leaving this prayer room until I do."

Knock, and Keep on Knocking

In Luke chapter 18, you can read about the woman and the unjust judge. She had more wisdom than most of us! That woman just kept knocking. The unjust judge told her to go away, but she kept knocking until he answered her. Well, we have to keep knocking too. God is not unjust, but we have to learn how to be consistent and steady when we're dealing with life's adversities.

You may have something you're knocking on today — some kind of problem or adversity. You may be dealing with some problem in your family, your finances, or your body. If you are, get alone with the Lord. It's good to read good teaching books and listen to good tapes, but stop doing all that and get your Bible. Talk to the Lord about your situation. Say, "Lord, I've had enough of this, and I know You can do something about it. Now I am going to stay with You and Your Word. I want You to talk to me and show me what to do."

Now remember, you can't always understand the Lord with your mind. You can't lean to your own understanding, because it may be the silliest thing that He tells you to do.

Whatsoever God Tells *You* — Do It!

I already showed you John 6:63, which says, "*. . .the words that I speak unto YOU, they are spirit, and they are life.*" I emphasized that word "you," because it is a personal thing. In other words, the words He does *not* speak to you, or the words you *don't permit* Him to speak to you, are not going to be Spirit and life, and they are not going to be anointed. They are not going to produce any result.

I want to further illustrate that point. Look at John chapter 2 at the account of the wedding at Cana. The hosts ran out of wine and needed some more. I want you to pay special attention to the instructions that Mary, Jesus' mother, gave to the servants.

JOHN 2:3-10
3 And when they wanted wine, the mother of Jesus saith unto him, They have no wine.
4 Jesus saith unto her, Woman, what have I to do with thee? mine hour is not yet come.
5 His mother saith unto the servants, WHATSOEVER HE SAITH UNTO YOU, do it.
6 And there were set there six waterpots of stone, after the manner of the purifying of the Jews, containing two or three firkins apiece.
7 Jesus saith unto them, Fill the waterpots with water. And they filled them up to the brim.
8 And he saith unto them, Draw out now, and bear unto the governor of the feast. And they bare it.
9 When the ruler of the feast had tasted the water that was made wine, and knew not whence it was: (but the servants which drew the water knew;) the governor of the feast called the bridegroom,
10 And saith unto him, Every man at the beginning doth set forth good wine; and when men have well drunk, then that which is worse: but thou hast kept the good wine until now.

Now this is the account of the miracle of Jesus' turning the water into wine, but *your* miracle is in verse 5: ". . . .*Whatsoever he saith unto you, DO IT*"!

Mary said this to the wedding servants, and a miracle took place. Those same words of wisdom are *your* key to pressing in to receive your miracle: Whatever, Jesus saith unto you, *do it*!

Chapter 7

The Difference Between A Voice and an Echo

The difference between an echo and a voice is simply this: An echo is just an "after-effect." We know that's true in the natural. Well, spiritually, a person speaking with an echo might *hear* the Word of God, and he may even *sense* the *power* of God. But the Word is not abiding in his spirit, and when he speaks, the power has already come and gone, so to speak. There is no power in his words. He may have heard the Word, but the Word is not in him, in his spirit. So his words are just an echo of the life and power that's in the Word of God.

An echo is empty. When you speak with an echo in the natural, the "power" or voice of your words is already gone by the time you hear the sound of the echo.

An echo is just a reflection of a voice!

On the other hand, a voice is a right-now voice that carries the authority, ability, weight, and power of God! It carries the might of God! It is a word from God spoken from your mouth that produces power!

Did you ever notice in Jesus' earthly ministry that many times, He got instant results? Now waiting for a manifestation is all right in itself. But we have been *training* ourselves to wait!

I believe that some things you're believing for, you won't have to *wait* for if you have enough "*weight*" in your words! When you speak the Word of God with the voice of Jesus, it will cut down the waiting period, and the manifestation will come *now* — right away.

We've been endeavoring to constantly hold fast to our confession. That's good; that's Scripture. But there are some things that God wants us to know so we can have certain situations and circumstances obey us *immediately*.

But in order to do that, you've got to have a voice. You can't just have an echo and get results with the Word.

Characteristics of a Voice

What are some of the characteristics of someone with a voice? For one, there is a certain confidence in him. There is an authority. There is an ability. There is a weight. And there is a power.

Just think about some problem — maybe it's a problem in your home — and then think about speaking to that problem with a voice. Or maybe it's a financial situation. With a voice instead of an echo, you can go with assurance and confidence to God and say, "Father, I thank Thee that Thou hast heard me" (John 11:41).

And they won't be just words with you. You're speaking with the voice of Jesus, and *you know that you know that you know* that what you are about to say is already true and *will* come to pass. You will be full of confidence and boldness and the spirit of faith. You have the sword of the Spirit, and you know God cannot deny His Word. He told us He watches over it to perform it (Jer. 1:12). He also said, "My Word will not return to Me void; it shall accomplish — it shall prosper in — whatever I send it to do" (Isa. 55:11).

So when you have a voice, you know what will happen before you even say it. You're just saying it to make a demand on it, because you're in the natural realm, and you have to appropriate or possess in this realm what is legally yours. Your spirit is already in the supernatural, creative ability of God. That's what it means to speak with the voice of Jesus. And when you speak with a voice, you know your words have creative power. That which does not exist, your words are powerful enough to bring it on the scene, because you're talking in the supernatural.

Walking in this is more than just being a church member. It's being a child of God who is walking in the Word and who knows who he is in Christ. He knows who the Holy Ghost, the Greater One, is on the inside of him. He knows the power of faith and love. And when it comes to receiving answers from the Word, he cannot be denied!

You know, I can't be broke. Satan may attack me; he may persecute me. He comes against me, all right. But he can't stay. I'm too far gone in the Word to ever be broke another day in my life! I have a voice — a rhema — in the area of prosperity.

The Process and the Product

There is a process to receiving the product or result of your faith in the abiding Word. The *abiding Word* produces the *spirit of faith*. The *spirit of faith* releases the *sword of the Spirit*. The *sword of the Spirit* releases the *authority, ability, weight, and power of God*. It is a *process*.

I want you to remember that, because you may be going through things now that you don't understand. But, remember, *the process is on its way to the product*. The process you are going through, if you handle it right, is always on its way to the product!

You see, in the area of finances, God has been "processing" me for twenty-two years. I'm at the product stage now. That's why I can stand before people and tell them I am a long way from broke. I have a beautiful wife and four happy, prosperous children. I live in a nice house and drive a nice car. I'm the biggest tither and biggest giver in my church.

There's no way around this divine process that I'm talking about. In other words, you can't just go to speaking before you've been abiding — before you have a rhema. We all have the written Word, but a lot of times, we've been trying to get the written Word to do only what a rhema — a *spoken* word — can do. When you speak the Word of God with the anointing, the power of the Holy Ghost rolls in. The wind blows, the fire burns, and the rain falls!

As I said before, all of the Word of God is the sword of the Spirit according to Ephesians 6:17, but all of the Word of God is not necessarily the sword of the Spirit to *you*. All of the Word of God has the *ability* to be a rhema, a spoken word from God directly to you that you can use as a sword. The entire Word of God has the *potential* and even the *probability* of being a rhema, but all of it is not at any given moment automatically a rhema or sword of the Spirit to *you*.

John 15:7 says, *"If ye abide in me, and my words abide in you, ye shall ask what ye will, and it shall be done unto you."* That's where the revelation comes from concerning the things that God has already provided for you. By your abiding in Christ and allowing the Word to abide in you, you can come to know for yourself the things that rightfully and legally belong to you.

Refuse To Do Without!

When you have the revelation from the Word of what belongs to you in Christ, you will refuse to do without. You'll also have the ability to make an impact in the spiritual realm to cause that which you know is yours to come to pass. Why? Because you're speaking the Word of God with the voice of Jesus!

Listen, friend, the reason we've been waiting so long — praying about things and confessing about things so long — is, we have been echoing. One of the reasons we've been echoing is, we've been using stale manna.

Fresh Manna and a Fresh Anointing

I know it; you know it; we all know it's true. As I said before, we can't deal with situations and circumstances with a "dead" word — one that hasn't been quickened to us. So we might as well do something about it and receive fresh manna, a fresh word, for the situations we're dealing with. If we don't, our situations are going to remain the same.

For example, Philippians 4:19 says, *"But my God shall supply all your need according to his riches in glory by Christ Jesus,"* but many people who are confessing that are still broke. Why? Because that scripture is not fresh to them. They are speaking with an echo and not a voice.

Don't get upset with me if you've been confessing long and waiting long, but you're still short on results. I'm teaching this to help you change that. You need a fresh word from God in your spirit. *When He gives you a fresh word and that word comes back out of your spirit through your mouth, it becomes the voice of Jesus speaking!* Satan, mountains, problems, situations and circumstances won't hear you anymore. They'll hear Jesus! Why? Because your words will take on the characteristics or the authority, ability, weight, and power of Jesus' words.

Turn to Acts 19. I'm going to teach you in greater detail the difference between a voice and an echo. It is a fact that many Christians have been echoing. They are good Christians. They love the Lord and His Word, but they've been echoing. The reason I know that is that echoing doesn't get results like a voice will.

You'd just as well tell yourself the truth if that applies to you. The sooner you tell yourself the truth, the sooner you can begin to turn some things around in your life. You need to write down the things you've just been "echoing" about instead of speaking about with a voice. You need to ask yourself the question, "In the situations I'm dealing with in my life now, am I a voice or an echo?"

> **ACTS 19:11-16**
> **11 And God wrought special miracles by the hands of Paul:**
> **12 So that from his body were brought unto the sick handkerchiefs or aprons, and the diseases departed from them, and the evil spirits went out of them.**
> **13 Then certain of the vagabond Jews, exorcists, took upon them to call over them which had evil spirits the name of the Lord Jesus, saying, We adjure you by Jesus whom Paul preacheth.**
> **14 And there were seven sons of one Sceva, a Jew, and chief of the priests, which did so.**
> **15 And the evil spirit answered and said, Jesus I know, and Paul I know; but who are ye?**
> **16 And the man in whom the evil spirit was leaped on them, and overcame them, and prevailed against them, so that they fled out of that house naked and wounded.**

Before I go any further, look at verse 13: *"Then certain of the vagabond Jews, exorcists, TOOK UPON THEM* [took upon themselves] *to call over them which had evil spirits the name of the Lord Jesus . . . ."*

Don't Take It Upon Yourself To Exercise Authority — Speak With a Voice Instead!

In much the same way those vagabond Jews took it upon themselves to exercise authority in the Name of Jesus, a lot of people are just taking it upon themselves to use scriptures they are not acquainted with to try to deal with something. The Holy Ghost didn't tell them to use those scriptures, but they're taking it upon themselves to use them rather than to seek the Lord and let the Word of God abide in them. They are using those verses because Kenneth Copeland used them, Jerry Savelle used them, Kenneth Hagin used them, or Fred Price used them. (I know this sounds "heavy," but if you'll pay attention, you can walk away from reading this and be loaded with confidence in God's Word for yourself.)

Notice from Acts 19:13 how an echo sounds.

> **ACTS 19:13**
> **13 Then certain of the vagabond Jews, exorcists, took upon them to call over them which had evil spirits the name of the Lord Jesus, saying, WE ADJURE YOU by Jesus WHOM PAUL PREACHETH.**

Notice the vagabond Jews were adjuring those evil spirits by Jesus "whom Paul preacheth." The authority that's in the Name of Jesus was real to Paul; it was a rhema. But it wasn't real to these other people. They were just echoing what they'd heard Paul and others say.

Now I'm going to show you echo results in verses 13 through 16, which talk about the seven sons of Sceva.

> **ACTS 19:13-16**
> **13 Then certain of the vagabond Jews, exorcists, took upon them to call over them which had evil spirits the name of the Lord Jesus, saying, We adjure you by Jesus whom Paul preacheth.**
> **14 And there were seven sons of one Sceva, a Jew, and chief of the priests, which did so.**
> **15 And the evil spirit answered and said, Jesus I know, and Paul I know; but who are ye?**
> **16 And the man in whom the evil spirit was leaped on them, and overcame them, and prevailed against them, so that they fled out of that house naked and wounded.**

Actually, the results the seven sons received are the same results a lot of people in the Body of Christ have been receiving. They go out and "echo" at the devil and make him mad enough to "whip their tails," but they don't have any authority to stop him. The devil says, "That's an echo. I don't have to listen to this."

Notice in verse 15, the evil spirit recognized the fact that those seven brothers were just echoes. That spirit knew they didn't have any authority over him. The evil spirit answered them, ". . . *Jesus I know, and Paul I know; but who are ye?*"

The Devil Is Stopped in His Tracks
At the Sound of a Voice

Some believers today are echoing at the devil, and he knows they're just echoing. Then some demons get together and say, "Let's answer them," and those believers don't have enough power to stop them!

I know the enemy will come against the Word or come against a believer for the Word's sake. But a lot of times, the devil comes too far for me to believe a person is really using the Word.

For example, someone might *say* he's using the rhema word, but the devil is coming too far for that person to really be using the rhema word. The devil is overcoming him and prevailing against him, just like he did those seven sons in Acts 19:16.

ACTS 19:16
16 And the man in whom the evil spirit was leaped on them, and overcame them, and prevailed against them, so that they fled out of that house naked and wounded.

Why did the devil overcome and prevail against the seven sons of Sceva? Because they were an echo; they weren't a real voice. That's the reason the devil can defeat a person who says he's using the Word but really isn't.

The devil can tell if you're an echo. If you are just echoing at the devil, he will know that you're not a voice. And he'll answer you, "Come on, let's deal with it, then."

He'll come at you with more pressure, and you won't be able to handle it, because you don't have a foundation in the Word to stand on. You've substituted pet scriptures and phrases you've picked up from somebody else for scriptures *God* wants to give you! Therefore, when the pressure comes, you don't have the authority, ability, weight, and power to withstand the pressure and enter into victory.

Don't Compound Your Problems

You know, a person could have some kind of problem to start with and get more problems besides that one if the enemy finds out he doesn't really have what he says he has. If the person says he has a voice but really doesn't, more problems will come against him, because he's saying or speaking out what he doesn't really have. In other words, the abiding Word is not in his spirit. He doesn't have a rhema, and the devil knows it. Too many people have been saying, "We're the head and not the tail," and their tails are dragging all the time!

For example, in the area of money, the Body of Christ in general is broke — *too* broke! Many are confessing this and confessing that. Certainly, I believe in confession, but with all their *confessing, confessing, confessing,* it looks like something ought to be *manifesting, manifesting, manifesting!*

Let's read Acts 19:13-15 again.

> **ACTS 19:13-15**
> **13 Then certain of the vagabond Jews, exorcists, took upon them to call over them which had evil spirits the name of the Lord Jesus, saying, We adjure you by Jesus whom Paul preacheth.**
> **14 And there were seven sons of one Sceva, a Jew, and chief of the priests, which did so.**
> **15 And the evil spirit ANSWERED and said, Jesus I know, and Paul I know; but who are ye?**

Evil spirits answer echoes. For example, if you were quoting, "My God shall supply all my need according to His riches in glory by Christ Jesus," but that verse wasn't real to you, the evil spirit might say, "Oh, yeah. You're going to *stay* broke, because you're just quoting scriptures. That's not a rhema to you."

Has God said to you, "I am your supplier"? Have you spent a little time with Him so He could say directly to you from His Word, "I am the supplier of all of your needs"? Do you have that verse in you so deep that you can't even *think* broke?

'Who Are *You*?'

Listen to what the evil spirit said in verse 15, "... *Jesus I know* [He has a voice], *and Paul I know* [he has a voice]; *but who are ye* [you're an echo]*?*" In other words, that spirit said, "Paul has a voice; I'm not messing with him. But who are you — you're just an echo!"

In the face of pressures and tests and trials, you need to make sure you have a voice! As a matter of fact, you're better off not saying *anything* to a particular situation than to speak to it with an echo. You need to talk the Word to *yourself* until you have a *voice*.

You see, the first part of confession is for *you*, to get that Word in your spirit where it can abide and become a rhema (actually, *most of the time*, confession is for you).

But many times, we take confession and immediately begin dealing with the devil and the situation with it. What we need to do first is to let the Word talk to us until it becomes a rhema.

This happens by your meditating the Word and repeating it to yourself. Then when it becomes a rhema, you speak it out one more time, and things will start coming to pass!

Now this is what has been happening to many Christians. They come out of religion and tradition, and they are whipped and defeated. Then they learn a little bit about faith and new-creation realities. Now they're *bad*! (You know what I mean by that — they think they're really something, a faith *giant*!) They've learned a little bit, and they immediately go to echoing. They've got a whole set of confessions, but they're just echoing.

We saw previously that if you're just an echo, the devil or an evil spirit will answer, just as the evil spirit answered the seven sons of Sceva in verse 15. But then look at verse 16.

ACTS 19:16
16 And the man in whom the evil spirit was LEAPED ON THEM, and OVERCAME THEM, and PREVAILED AGAINST THEM, so that they fled out of that house naked and wounded.

When you speak the Word of God to your problem before you're ready — before you really know what you're talking about — your problem is not going to leave you; it's going to *leap on* you!

I've experienced this in the past in my own life, and I know this happens with many Christians. For example, they're paying tithes and praying, but they're still broke (and some of them get even "broker"). Why? Because Malachi 3:10 is not a revelation to them: *"Bring ye all the tithes into the storehouse, that there may be meat in mine house, and prove me now herewith, saith the Lord of hosts, if I will not open you the windows of heaven, and pour you out a blessing, that there shall not be room enough to receive it."*

When that verse becomes a revelation to you, you will know that the windows of Heaven are open to you. You will just expect promotion and prosperity in whatever way the Lord brings it. You will know that "Money cometh" works!

Acts 19:16 says, "... *the man in whom the evil spirit was leaped on them, and overcame them, and prevailed against them. ...*" You see, an echo puts you in the position to be leaped on, overcome, and prevailed over. But on the other side of that is a voice!

Look at what happens when you speak with a voice.

ACTS 19:20
20 So mightily grew the word of God and prevailed.

When you are a voice, that's what happens — the Word of God will prevail in your life over whatever it is you are dealing with.

Defeated No More!

Your grasping these truths can change your life before your very eyes. There's power in the abiding, anointed, rhema Word of God! Instead of looking at your circumstances, whipped and defeated, you will rise up and stand up to that situation and declare, "I'm not an echo; I'm a voice. And whatever I talk to has to obey me just like it would obey Jesus!"

We as Christians are the Body of Christ. John 15:7 is the principle Jesus showed us whereby we could become a voice: *"If ye abide in me, and my words abide in you, ye shall ask what ye will, and it shall be done unto you."* Through this verse, Jesus showed us the power He operated in while He was on the earth.

You know, God actually meant for the Body of Christ to be living a lifestyle of people who are blessed and happy. Jesus ministered three years *before* the Cross to show us how we should live and minister on the *other side* of the Cross. Jesus tarried those three years as a man operating under the anointing of the Holy Spirit to show us something. He showed us how to speak the Word of God in faith and with the anointing of God upon it to bring results on the scene!

Some people say, "Yes, but He was the Son of God." Yes, He was the Son of God, but in Philippians we find that Jesus stripped Himself of His mighty glory and power (Phil. 2:6-8). He had to become a man in order to die for us. I know He had the Spirit without measure (John 3:34) during His earthly ministry. But by the same token, you have the ability to do what Jesus did in the Gospels. If you didn't, we would have to take John 14:12 out of the Bible.

> **JOHN 14:12**
> 12 Verily, verily, I say unto you, He that believeth on me, the works that I do shall he do also; and greater works than these shall he do; because I go unto my Father.

According to John 14:12, God expects us to do what Jesus did. Jesus Himself said we could do greater things. But in order to do those things, we have to learn to operate in the

Word like Jesus operated. We've got to get John 15:7 working in *our* lives like Jesus had it working in *His* life.

You Need the *Word* of God
To Do the *Works* of God

Now someone who is not a student of the Word might think I'm being sacreligious or disrespectful of Jesus, but all I'm saying is what Jesus Himself said! You see, we are the Body of Christ. Why would He call us His Body? Because He has given us collectively the same anointing that He had individually. We have the same Holy Spirit who anointed Jesus, and we have the same works to do, and even more, because Jesus said, *". . . the works that I do shall he do also; AND GREATER WORKS THAN THESE SHALL HE DO; because I go unto my Father."*

Well, you can't do the *works* of God without the *Word* of God!

Look again at John 14:10.

JOHN 14:10
10 Believest thou not that I am in the Father, and the Father in me? the words that I speak unto you I speak not of myself: but the Father that dwelleth in me, he doeth the works.

In the fourteenth chapter, Jesus revealed to the disciples how He was doing everything that He did. *All the works of Jesus were done by the Word.* Did you get that? It is the Word that doeth the work!

Jesus' authority rested in the fact that He didn't move without a word from His Father — not a word from Ezekiel, Jeremiah, or one of the apostles. No, Jesus got a word from *the Father.*

Actually, John 14:10 and John 15:7 are "first cousins." Let me explain that. In a conversation with Phillip, Jesus said, *"Believest thou not that I AM IN THE FATHER, and* the FATHER IN ME? *the words that I speak unto you I speak not of myself: but* THE FATHER THAT DWELLETH IN ME, HE DOETH THE WORKS" (John 14:10).

In John 14:10, Jesus said, "Believest thou not that I am in the Father?" Then notice the next part of His question: ". . . *and the Father* [is] *in me?. . .*" Can you could see the parallel revelation between this verse and John 15:7? Jesus was saying in John 14:10, "Everything I'm doing, I'm doing because I heard My Father say it. Then I said it, and that's why it happened."

Jesus said something similar in John 15:7: *"If ye abide in me, and my words abide in you, ye shall ask what ye will, and it shall be done unto you."*

I'll make that clearer to you by reading John 8:28: *"Then said Jesus unto them, When ye have lifted up the Son of man, then shall ye know that I am he, and that I do nothing of myself; but as my Father hath taught me, I speak these things."*

What was Jesus saying? He was saying, "I say what the Father says unto Me. The reason I say something is, the Father has said it to Me. I have the voice of My Father. Therefore, what I talk to must obey Me, because it's no longer Me talking but the Father"!

What we have to do is say what the Father is saying to *us* so we can have the Father Himself "speaking" out of our mouth!

Look at John 12:49.

JOHN 12:49
49 For I have not spoken of myself; but the Father which sent me, he gave me a commandment [a word], what I should say, and what I should speak.

Notice the first words; ". . . *I have not spoken of myself. . . .*"

You see, when you are echoing, you are speaking "of yourself." You don't have a rhema from God. You are speaking something you want to say or that you think is right.

Follow Jesus' Example — Work the Word, and the Word Will Do the Work!

If we are going to receive a rhema word from God and speak with a voice like Jesus did, we are going to have to follow Jesus' example.

> **JOHN 14:10-14**
> **10 Believest thou not that I am in the Father, and the Father in me? the words that I speak unto you I speak not of myself: but the Father that dwelleth in me, he doeth the works.**
> **11 Believe me that I am in the Father, and the Father in me: or else believe me for the very works' sake.**
> **12 Verily, verily, I say unto you, He that believeth on me, the works that I do shall he do also; and greater works than these shall he do; because I go unto my Father.**
> **13 And whatsoever ye shall ask in my name, that will I do, that the Father may be glorified in the Son.**
> **14 If ye shall ask any thing in my name, I will do it.**

In verse 12, Jesus is actually saying, "If you work the Word, the Word will do the work!" He was talking about working the Word so that the Word may release the power to get the job done.

Then in verses 13 and 14, He explains the *result* of speaking the Word of God with supernatural power.

Jesus worked the Word like I'm telling you that *you* need to work it so that it can become alive and living in you. Jesus proved out in His own life and example why the Word worked for Him. It can work for you the same way! Jesus did not tell us to do anything that He had not already laid the format for. Speaking the Word of God with the voice of Jesus is based on John 15:7. Jesus abided in the Father like He told us to abide in Him. When Jesus spoke, the words that came out of His mouth were not His own words. They were the Father's words. Jesus had to have a relationship and a certain fellowship with the Father to speak like He did.

Read John 14:10 again. Jesus was saying, in effect, "I'm not doing on My own what you see being done. I'm only speaking what I heard My Father say. And because I'm speaking what I heard My Father say, I don't have to try to *make* it happen. It happens because My Father said for it to happen. I repeat what He said, and then My Father does the work."

The Power Is Already in the Seed of the Word

You see, once the Word becomes a rhema and a sword of the Spirit to you, you don't have to try to get it to fulfill itself. It is fulfilled as soon as you speak it! Why? Because you have the relationship and the fellowship going, and your words have a force behind them that is going to cause them to come to pass. *The power of the Word to make it come to pass is within the Word itself!* That's why the Word is often called the *seed*.

Not Automatic But Attainable

Jesus' voice was the voice of God, because Jesus spoke only what He heard the Father speak. We can operate in that realm too. It is not automatic, but it *is* attainable.

I'm going to share with you five things that caused Jesus to have a voice: 1) *He abided in the Father*; 2) *the Father abided in Him*; 3) *He abided in the Father's Word*; 4) *the Father spoke to Him;* and 5) *Jesus in turn spoke out that rhema word, giving the Father permission or access to manifest His ability and do the work!*

That's what can happen when you get a rhema, brother and sister! When you get a rhema, you have a voice. You can open your mouth and use the sword of the Spirit, and your words will pack weight with the devil, demons, mountains, and situations and circumstances. You'll be "packing it" when you have a rhema!

I was in the streets before I was saved, and we used to have a saying when nobody would mess with you that you were "*packing.*" Nobody messed with me when I was in the streets. Those boys would say, "Don't mess with him, man. He's *packing.*" That meant I was really tough!

Now, spiritually, I'm "packing"! When I go into a church, the devil and demons say, "Look out for him; he's *packing.*" (Whenever you call a preacher in who's not scared to let the Lord use him, partner, your church will get blessed!)

I hope you understand by now the vast difference between speaking the Word without a rhema and speaking it with the voice of Jesus!

Let's look at one more aspect of speaking the Word of God with the voice of Jesus. This is what I call the "icing" on everything I've taught in this book so far.

'It Is Written' Versus 'It Is Said'

Look at Luke the fourth chapter to see again the voice of Jesus in operation.

LUKE 4:1-3
1 And Jesus being full of the Holy Ghost returned from Jordan, and was led by the Spirit into the wilderness,
2 Being forty days tempted of the devil. And in those days he did eat nothing: and when they were ended, he afterward hungered.
3 And the devil said unto him, If thou be the Son of God, command this stone that it be made bread.

Notice what Jesus said to the devil.

LUKE 4:4
4 And Jesus answered him, saying, IT IS WRITTEN, That man shall not live by bread alone, but by every word of God.

Notice those three words "It is written." Now what was Jesus talking about — "It is written"? It is written that "man shall not live by bread alone, but by every word of God"!

> **LUKE 4:5**
> **5 And the devil, taking him up into an high mountain, shewed unto him all the kingdoms of the world in a moment of time.**

You see, the devil doesn't just quit because you quote a few scriptures. He will try to keep messing with you.

> **LUKE 4:6**
> **6 And the devil said unto him, All this power will I give thee, and the glory of them: for that is delivered unto me; and to whomsoever I will I give it.**

The devil had a right to say that: "All this power will I give . . . ." You see, he is the god of this world (2 Cor. 4:4). He has certain power, because he's the god of this world. Adam was originally in charge but fell short and sold himself out to the devil. That's how the devil became the god of this world.

That's why you see some devilish folks who look like they're faring well. They don't serve God, yet they look like they're doing pretty well. That's the devil. He's the god of this world, and he's their father. He's letting them have the stuff they have. He's trying to keep it out of the Kingdom of God, so he lets devilish people have money who will hoard it for themselves and drive fancy cars.

Now I drive a nice car. But I tell you, I wouldn't want a car if I had to be devilish in order to have it. There's nothing of eternal value in having a nice car. If I had to choose, I'd let all that other stuff go — I want Jesus!

So the devil said to Jesus, ". . .*All this power will I give thee, and the glory of them: for that is delivered unto me; and to whomsoever I will I give it*" (Luke 4:6).

LUKE 4:7,8
7 If thou therefore wilt worship me, all shall be thine.
8 And Jesus answered and said unto him, Get thee behind me, Satan: for IT IS WRITTEN, Thou shalt worship the Lord thy God, and him only shalt thou serve.

There they are again — those three words "It is written." Notice that Jesus said, "It is written" twice (vv. 4,8). Then notice in verse 10, the devil says it too: "It is written." He is using Scripture to try to trip Jesus up!

LUKE 4:9,10
9 And he brought him [Jesus] to Jerusalem, and set him on a pinnacle of the temple, and said unto him, If thou be the Son of God, cast thyself down from hence:
10 For IT IS WRITTEN, He shall give his angels charge over thee, to keep thee.

Now Jesus had already said, "It is written" two times. In verse 10, I imagine the devil thought, *I can say it too*. And he did. He quoted a passage from the Psalms: "*. . . he shall give his angels charge over thee, to keep thee in all thy ways*" (Ps. 91:11).

Quotes Are Just Echoes

So that's the third time in this passage we've seen "It is written." The third time, it was the devil who said, "It is written" and quoted Scripture. But anybody can make a quote — quotes are just echoes.

When the devil used the scripture recorded in verse 11, I can imagine Jesus saying, "I need to pull out a 'rhema' here. I'm going to stop talking about what is written now. I am out of his class, so I'm going to change My conversation about what is in the Bible and what is *written* and start talking to him about what is *said*. Instead of just talking about what God's Word says, I'm going to talk about what God's Word is saying to *Me*."

LUKE 4:12,13
12 And Jesus answering said unto him, IT IS SAID, Thou shalt not tempt the Lord thy God.
13 And when the devil had ended all the temptation, he departed from him for a season.

Goodness! In verse 10, Satan began to make quotes, but then Jesus pulled out a sword!

I can just imagine Jesus saying, "Listen here, devil. I've told you some things God has said, but 'It is written' is not working with you. Let's stop quoting scriptures now, so I can *really* start speaking. In My mouth is a two-edged sword! It is *said!*"

Another Level in Spiritual Warfare

Can you see the shift Jesus made in His temptation by the devil? It was as if Jesus was saying, "Look, we're not going to talk anymore about what's in the Scripture; we're going to talk about what's abiding in *Me*. I'm going to talk to you about what is Spirit and life. I'm going to talk out of the spirit of faith that is within Me."

You see, when Satan began echoing the Word of God, Jesus said, in effect, "I can't talk to you on this level. I'm going to another level in this conversation. I've been talking about what is written, but I'm going to start talking about what is *said!*"

You see, Satan could say, "It is written" all day long, but Jesus had "It is written" on the inside of Him — in His heart! He had a rhema for the devil. Jesus pulled out a sword!

Satan will try to mess with Christians who are saying, "It is written." That's why they'd better know what they really believe. "It is written" ought to be more than just "It is written" to them. It ought to be "It is *said.*" It ought to be a rhema to them. But if they are just an echo, Satan will really mess with them.

Jesus didn't have any problem answering or following up behind Satan when he started quoting the Word. He probably said, "Wait a minute — wait just a minute! Let's see you follow *this*! I'm going to talk to you about a rhema now. Let Me see if you've got any rhema in *you*! Let Me see if *you've* heard from God."

Use the Word as Your Weapon

Jesus pulled a sword out on the devil! The devil found out that Jesus knew what He was talking about when He was quoting the Scripture. Jesus wasn't just quoting it out of His head; He was talking about what was spoken directly to Him by God and about that which had become rhema to Him. And the devil had to obey. Jesus knew that. He could "cut the devil up" with that sword of the Spirit.

When Jesus used the Word against the devil, that Word was not just something Jesus heard once or twice. No, that Word was something down on the inside of Him that produced in Him authority, ability, weight, and power.

Satan Can't Receive a Rhema

So "It is written" is different than "It is said." Do you see that? The whole Bible is *written* to you, but when you get a *voice*, you can say, "It has been *spoken* to me!" Satan can't handle "It is said," because he never heard what was said. God was not talking to him; God was talking to the person who was seeking Him. God gave that person a rhema, and, suddenly, "It is *written*" became "It is *said*."

Someone might ask, "How could Satan quote the Word?" Well, he knew the Bible, because he was with God at first before he rebelled and fell like lightning from Heaven (Luke 10:18). Of course, the devil can't receive revelation knowledge and use the sword of the Spirit, but he knows how to quote the Word. That's why just saying, "It is written" to the devil is not going to work with him if what is written is not in your heart — if it hasn't become "It is *said*" to you.

The devil can't say, "It is said." He only can say, "It is written," because God is not talking to him anymore. But we can have a rhema, a spoken word of God, just for us when we need it. We can pull out the sword of the Spirit. The devil does not have a sword of the Spirit, but we do. That's why we can whip him every time.

In Luke 4:4, Jesus said, ". . . *It is WRITTEN, That man shall not live by bread alone, but by every word of God.*" Then again in verse 8, Jesus said, ". . . *IT IS WRITTEN, Thou shalt worship the Lord thy God, and him only shalt thou serve.*"

Then in verse 10, the *devil* says, "It is written" too. One thing you can learn from this is, if you don't have a rhema, you and the devil are on equal footing to a certain extent. You can quote or echo scriptures to him, and he's going to quote scriptures back to you!

But with a rhema word from God, you can do what Jesus did. When the devil quoted Scripture to Jesus in Luke 4:10 and 11, Jesus immediately shifted gears on the devil. Jesus pulled out the sword of the Spirit! He quit saying, "It is *written*" and told the devil, "It is *said*" (v. 12)!

Listen, the devil quoted Scripture to Jesus, and that's exactly what the devil will do to *you*. So you've got to be able to pull out that sword and say to the devil, "Not is it only *written*, but it has been *said* to me that I'm the head and not the tail! It's been *said* to me that God shall supply all my needs. Devil, I'm not talking about what is written; I'm talking about what has been spoken to *me*, what is alive in my spirit."

That's what the devil understands. You might mess around awhile saying, "It is written," but when you speak that which is written because it has been *said* to you by God, the devil's day of harassing you is over!

You Are Satan's Master

Notice Jesus changed from saying, "It is *written*" to "It is *said*." Jesus had a rhema word; He was out of the devil's class. And when *you* have a rhema word, you will be out of the devil's class too. When you know what is spoken directly to you, you are out of his class. He can't go another round with you, so to speak. He has to put his gloves down. You have become his master.

That's the way it should be in your life. The devil needs to know that you know what you're talking about when you stand against him with the Word. He needs to know that you are his master. He needs to know that the Word on the inside of you is Spirit and life. He needs to know that you're anointed and that you can destroy His works (*see* First John 3:8; John 14:12).

The Enemy's Echoes
Are No Match for Your Voice!

You can cut the devil with the sword, but he can't cut you. He doesn't have a sword. Actually, because you have the sword of the Spirit, you are fighting an enemy who can't fight with you! He doesn't have anything to cut with!

Some people need to stop giving the devil all the credit. The devil is no match for a born-again, Spirit-filled, Word-changed, sword-swinging Christian! The devil can't stop you. He can't hold you down. He can't hold you back, because you heard what God said: "You are My child. Wherever you go, I am with you always" (Matt. 28:20; Heb. 13:5).

You can have a voice! You don't have to be an echo. You can have a voice that Satan can't deny. He's got to obey you when you have a voice. When you get the Word of God abiding inside you, revelation knowledge comes out of you. You begin operating in the spirit of faith, and you have a voice that Satan has to obey. He can't hold any sickness on you. He can't hold poverty on you. He can't cut you off early in life. He can't mess your family up — because when you speak, he must obey you!

Sometimes you need to just stand up and say, "Devil, who are you talking to? What do you mean by threatening me like that? Do you know whose I am?" When you have a voice, you will speak with confidence. When you have the sword of the Spirit, you don't care what the devil says. Let the wind blow and the billows rise; your ship can't go under!

There isn't any ship that's going to go down with me on it. I've got an anchor in me, holding that ship in place. What is my anchor? My anchor is this: I know whose I am, and my Father said that He would never leave me nor forsake me.

(In Acts 27, there is an account of a ship that did sink. Paul was on that ship, but Paul was not hurt, because he had an anchor, a rhema word from God.)

Determine that you're not going to be an echo but a voice. Satan has to obey you. With a voice — with a rhema word of God, the sword of the Spirit — say to him, "Satan, take your hands off my children. Take your hands off my spouse. Take your stinky hands off my money. You've got to obey me. Take your hands off my job. Take your hands off my business. Take your hands off my body.

"Who do you think you are? I have a voice. I say to you, 'With Jesus' stripes, I am healed.' I say to you, 'The Lord is my Shepherd, I shall not want.' I say to you, 'My God shall supply all of my needs according to His riches in glory by Christ Jesus.' I say to you, 'I am the head and not the tail.' Who do you think you are, devil? You can't say anything to me to hurt me; you're not on my level. You're under my feet. Jesus said to me, 'I give you power to tread upon serpents and scorpions and over the power of the enemy, and nothing shall by any means harm you.'"

This information I'm sharing is new to some people. Some of them don't want to receive it. My daddy used to raise cattle. Some of the cattle didn't always want to eat. My daddy would say, "Just let them go on to the pasture. If they don't want to eat, they just don't want to eat." That's true with some folks spiritually. They just don't want to eat anything new, so you just have to let them "go on to the pasture." But they can speak with a voice if they'll adhere to the Word of God.

Chapter 8

How To Speak the Word of God With the Voice of Jesus!

In this chapter, we're going to look in greater detail at the voice of Jesus. We want to learn how to turn our voice into the voice of Jesus. There are some things that we have to do to speak with the voice of Jesus, but it is possible for us to speak with the same authority and power, and experience the same results that Jesus experienced when He was here on the earth.

We'll look again at John chapter 15 to see why Jesus' words were so powerful. We'll find out why everything He spoke to always obeyed Him even though He operated on the earth, not as the Son of God but as a man anointed by the Holy Ghost (Matt. 3:16; Mark 1:10; Luke 3:22; 4:18; John 1:32).

There is nothing that the Lord Jesus spoke to that didn't obey Him. I said previously that He was setting a pattern on the *"before-side"* of the Cross of the lifestyle that He would provide for us *on* the Cross — the lifestyle that we could live and experience on the *other* side — the *"after-side"* of the Cross!

We know we're on the other side of the Cross; we're on the other side of the price being paid. We're on the other side — we have our redemption. We're delivered from the power of darkness. Now we are in the Kingdom of God's dear Son (Col. 1:13). Therefore, we have the ability to live a lifestyle like Jesus lived when He was on earth. In Him, we actually have the same power and authority that He had while He was on the earth. Jesus had the Spirit without measure (John 3:34), but we individually can speak with a measure of the same power and authority, and we can experience the same results He experienced.

I have pastored for the past twenty-two years and have traveled and ministered all over the country. I have seen many good people really working the Word and getting some results. But the Body of Christ as a whole is not getting consistent results like we should be getting.

A Voice Carries Spiritual Weight and Anointing — An Echo Is Lifeless and Empty

A pastor friend of mine was in a shopping center once with a mightily used minister and elder in the faith. My friend asked the elder minister, "Why are your messages so different? Why are your books different than the books of many other men of God? When you speak, your words and your messages just stand out — why is that?"

This man of God is not very talkative. (He follows the admonishment of the Bible, "Be slow to speak." The more mature you get, the slower you are to speak.) So he didn't answer my friend right away.

We need to learn that lesson. When someone asks you a question, you've got time to think about it. You don't have to just answer. And when you are waiting, you're giving the Holy Spirit time to "kick in" and give you the right words to speak.

Have you ever said something in haste, and it messed you up? You should have been slower to speak. Most of us have done that at some time or another.

Well, when this pastor friend of mine asked the man of God that question, the elder minister didn't answer right away. He was just looking around the shopping center! Finally, he said to my friend, "Son, I have a *voice*. Most ministers have an *echo*."

This pastor shared that incident with me and told me, "Leroy, you have a voice about prosperity. I have heard a lot of *echoes* about prosperity, but you have a *voice*." This pastor was a prosperity teacher himself, and when he heard me teach on "Money cometh!" he recognized that I had a voice on the subject and not just an echo.

The Inspiration of the Almighty Gives Understanding

Look again at my golden text, John 15:7: *"If ye abide in me, and my words abide in you, ye shall ask what ye will, and it shall be done unto you."* Why could Jesus make such a promise? Because when the Word begins to abide in you, and you begin to meditate in and spend time with the Word, your will becomes His will; therefore, His will becomes your will. And you understand what Job said: *". . .there is a spirit in man: and the inspiration of the Almighty giveth them understanding"* (Job 32:8).

There is a spirit in man that receives understanding from the Almighty. You see, you need revelation knowledge, understanding, wisdom, and obedience to walk in the Word properly. And all of this happens by your abiding in the Word. Then you shall ask what you will, and it shall be done unto you!

The Understanding of God's Word Will Give You the Confidence to Stake Your Claim!

You remember I said that the last part of John 15:7 — "ye shall ask what ye will" — actually means, "You shall make a demand on what is legally yours." You see, when you know something belongs to you, you won't hesitate to say so. You won't hesitate to stake your claim. For example, I know my car belongs to me. It's paid for; it's mine. I don't have any creditors talking to me about that car. I have the title; it's my car. And I wouldn't hesitate to say so if someone tried to take it from me!

Creditors could get upset at me if they wanted to, but that car is mine; it belongs to me. I drive what the Father wants me to drive. He paid for it. He pays for the gas and upkeep. Nobody comes driving up in my driveway talking about my being late on a note, because my car is paid for — it is legally mine.

You Have a Part To Play
In Obtaining Your Legal Rights

I said in previous chapters that the Word *in general* is not automatically a rhema word or the sword of the Spirit to you. You have a part to play. *You* have to do something. You have to make the Word of God yours. You make it yours by doing John 15:7.

Jesus also said, *"It is the spirit that quickeneth; the flesh profiteth nothing: the words that I speak unto you, they are spirit, and they are life"* (John 6:63). In other words, Jesus was saying, "My words, the words I speak unto you, carry My supernatural power and ability." Once the Lord speaks a power-carrying word to you, then *you* have to take up the sword of the Spirit and use it on your problems!

Look at Hebrews chapter 4.

> **HEBREWS 4:12**
> 12 For the word of God is quick, and powerful, and sharper than any twoedged sword, piercing even to the dividing asunder of soul and spirit, and of the joints and marrow, and is a discerner of the thoughts and intents of the heart.

I like the *Amplified* translation of that verse.

> **HEBREWS 4:12**
> 12 For the Word that God speaks is alive and full of power [making it active, operative, energizing, and effective]; it is sharper than any two-edged sword, penetrating to the dividing line of the breath of life (soul) and [the immortal]

spirit, and of joints and marrow [of the deepest parts of our nature], exposing and sifting and analyzing and judging the very thoughts and purposes of the heart.

God intended that the Word in your mouth be active, operative, energizing, and effective in your life so that the next time you speak to that thing you've been speaking to over and over again, you're not going to have to wait anymore. You've waited and waited in the past. But when you are operating in the abiding Word, that problem is going to have to go! It's going to have to go visit someone else, because you are moving in a new vein — into a deeper revelation, illumination, inspiration, and anointing of God's Word.

The first part of Hebrews 4:12 deals with the power of the Word of God. It says, ". . .*the Word that God speaks* is alive and full of power. . . ." That's the Word that Jesus spoke — the same Word that God spoke. And that Word was full of power.

You Can't Win When You're an Echo — You Can't *Lose* When You're a *Voice*!

Jesus had a voice. He wasn't just an echo. And John the Baptist had a voice. He was the voice of one crying in the wilderness, saying, "Prepare ye the way of the Lord!" (Matt. 3:3; Mark 1:3; Luke 3:4). The devil has a certain voice too. It's not like the voice of God, but it's a voice. So you can't make it in life with just an echo.

You need the Word of God firmly planted in your heart. The devil respects a voice that's based on the authority of God's holy written Word.

Jesus has a voice in the Kingdom of God, the Kingdom of light. The devil has a voice in the kingdom of darkness, because Adam gave it to him. You as a believer need to have the Word of God abiding in you until it becomes the sword of the Spirit. Then you, too, will have a voice. And when you speak, your voice will be like Jesus' voice. The devil won't be able to tell the difference between your voice and Jesus' voice. When the devil hears you speak, he hears Jesus speaking, because you are speaking the Word of God out of the anointing and not out of your flesh. The flesh profiteth nothing (John 6:63).

'Echo' Talk Can't Receive 'Voice' Benefits

You can't be a parakeet or a repeater of a voice and expect to receive "voice" benefits! You've got to get down deep in the Word and let the Word get deep into you. Then you'll be able to pull the sword of the Spirit out in a given situation and cut down your problem with the Word of God!

You remember in John chapter 11 the account of Martha, Mary, and their brother Lazarus. Lazarus was sick, and Jesus showed up after Lazarus was already dead. But that didn't make any difference to Jesus, because He was the resurrection (John 11:25)!

In your own life, it doesn't matter how far your problem may have already gone. Jesus doesn't have to "get there" early in order to help you. No, even at the last turn, He can turn it around for you.

> **JOHN 11:39-44**
> 39 Jesus said, Take ye away the stone. Martha, the sister of him that was dead, saith unto him, LORD, BY THIS TIME HE STINKETH: for HE HATH BEEN DEAD FOUR DAYS.
> 40 Jesus saith unto her, Said I not unto thee, that, if thou wouldest believe, thou shouldest see the glory of God?
> 41 Then they took away the stone from the place where the dead was laid. And Jesus lifted up his eyes, and said, Father, I thank thee that thou hast heard me.
> 42 And I knew that thou hearest me always: but because of the people which stand by I said it, that they may believe that thou hast sent me.
> 43 And when he thus had spoken, he cried with a loud voice, Lazarus, come forth.
> 44 And HE THAT WAS DEAD CAME FORTH, bound hand

**and foot with graveclothes: and his face was bound about
with a napkin. Jesus saith unto them, Loose him, and let
him go.**

I want you to see that Jesus had a *voice*, not an *echo*, that
produced results! Jesus said with a voice, "Lazarus, come
forth!" and he that was dead came forth!

You need to know how to develop yourself so that you, too,
can have a voice like Jesus had. You have to develop, not just
your spirit but your mind too. You have to have the Word in
your heart or spirit, and you have to renew your mind with
the Word (Rom. 12:1). Then when you have that voice, things
start turning — mountains and trees start being removed,
winds stop blowing, waves stop crashing, and storms cease!

When you really have a voice like Jesus had, it rains
when you say, "Rain," and it stops raining when you say,
"Stop raining." Sickness flees and demons tremble when you
go to talking. Money cometh to you when you go to talking
with a voice! Your family life is joy unspeakable and full of
glory. Your children obey you; they want to obey and do right!

I'm talking about a voice, the voice of Jesus. Someone
might ask, "How does the fact that Jesus had a voice affect
me? Is Jesus still here?" Yes, He's here *in you* if you are born
again!

When the Word of God is spoken to you, it's a rhema —
it's a command from God. God has given it especially to you,
and when you are armed in your spirit with that Word,
spiritually, you are "heavy." You have a voice. You are like
Ezekiel, Jeremiah, and others in the Bible who had a voice.
You become "heavy"with the authority, ability, weight, and
power that God has given you.

Get 'Loaded' With the Word!

I remember a time when I was in the world without God.
There were times I'd drink whiskey and get "loaded." I knew

I was loaded, because I'd tell anybody to get out of my way. Nobody messed with me when I was loaded. If they tried to, I'd say, "Who are you talking to? Get back!"

Well, it's the same way when, spiritually, you get "loaded" and heavy with the Word of God in your spirit. You become like a "drunk" man! In other words, you don't care what the devil is trying to do. You just walk up to him and say, "Look, you've got to flee! You've got to go!" You know who you are in Christ, and it turns you into a different man or woman.

I tell you, the Church needs to get "loaded"! We need to just get flat loaded and begin to move out in the power of the "supernaturalness" of God!

When you get to that place with the Word of God, there is an electrical, supernatural current of the Holy Ghost flowing out of you, because the Word of God is anointed. And that anointing will deal with your situations, and deliverance will come. You will speak to you circumstance — not four, five, ten, fifteen, or twenty times — but *one* time.

You'll say to that problem, "You're through!" You will be talking with the voice of Jesus, and that thing will obey you and leave your house or your job or wherever you are. And if you want to leave your job, but it looks impossible, that voice will take you to another job. That voice will take you places where you can't go on your own.

Are Your Words Returning Empty Or Full of Power and Victory?

Some people are content in life to be just an echo. But, as I said, an echo is a *reflection* of a voice; it's not a real voice. And it doesn't produce the same results that a voice produces. An echo says something, but its words are empty words. An echo parakeets or repeats something that it heard, but it doesn't really know for itself what was said.

Many people receive good teaching from the Word but remain echoes. They aren't getting any results; they're still down in their canyons and valleys. Have you ever heard an actual echo? You could be in the mountains and holler, "Yoo-hoo," and in the distance, "yoo-hoo" will talk back to you! It even sounds empty and distant.

The devil doesn't pay an echo any mind. You could holler, "Yoo-hoo, I'm full of faith. I'm blessed going in and blessed coming out." But if that fact isn't real to you in your heart, the devil will say, "That's an echo. That person doesn't know what he is talking about." But when you are in your canyon of tests, trials, and problems, and you speak the Word of God with the voice of Jesus, that canyon will do what you tell it to do. God's Word is Spirit and life. That canyon will rise up and become a highway!

Don't Be Dominated
By Senses and Circumstances

The only thing that can separate spirit, soul, and body is the Word of God (Heb. 4:12). When you get to abiding in the Word, that Word separates your spirit from your soul and body long enough for the spirit to get strong and dominate the soul and body. Selfishness leaves you. Other fleshly traits leave you too.

What happens is, your spirit is separated from your soul and body long enough for God to talk with your spirit. When your body and soul come back into play, so to speak, your spirit has already heard from Heaven, and your spirit says, "No! Don't start any mess; we're going *this* way, *God's* way. Shut up! I'm in charge now. I'm full of the Word. So, soul, be renewed! Body, be under subjection! Line up and follow me!"

When people do not abide in the Word, their soul runs them. They come with an unrenewed mind to church, and they've got a mess on their mind. They want to confess the Lord and His Word, but they've got a mess going on in their mind, and they sometimes confess that instead. Therefore, the Word doesn't work for them.

That's why you need to have the Word abiding in you. Just saying the Word is not going to do the job by itself. No, you need the anointed Word of God penetrating you — getting down on the inside — in your spirit, cleaning you, purging you, revealing Jesus to you, and showing you a "mirror" of who you are — because of Christ, not because of your own goodness. That Word of God in your spirit will keep pride out.

You know, the Bible says pride comes before a fall (Prov. 16:18). But when you get hold of the abiding Word of God, you won't be in pride. You will find that you are nothing without Him. Jesus said, "Without Me, you are nothing" (John 15:5). Actually, what He is saying is that without the Word, you are nothing, because the only thing that can "cut through" your problem and be effectual is the Word.

Get Rid of Your Hang-Ups!

I tell you, the Word will cut through and get rid of your hang-ups! You need to stay with the Word and let the Word work on you. Jesus said, ". . . *Man shall not live by bread alone, but by every word that proceedeth out of the mouth of God*" (Matt. 4:4). Pay attention to that. Jesus is talking about the rhema Word. He said that man (or woman) shall not just live physically but spiritually, too, by every word that proceeds from the mouth of God.

For a word to proceed out of your mouth and have the same effect as a word proceeding out of the mouth of God, you're going to have to be abiding in it. It's going to have to be a rhema. But if you spend time with the Word, you'll have it.

It's not just hearing the Word, my brother and sister, that causes a rhema to come. Certainly, faith comes by hearing (Rom. 10:17). But it's not just having the facts of God's Word mentally. It's having a deep, abiding revelation knowledge or understanding of that Word. For example, you know that you know that a particular verse is yours when you are truly abiding. You know, "That Word is mine; I'm healed! I'm healed because Jesus says I'm healed. And I'm rich! Jesus says I'm rich. I'll never be broke another day in my life. Jesus said, 'Money cometh!' So I know that money cometh to *me*!"

Those words "Money cometh!" are prophetic words. They're rhema words from Heaven that I received several years ago, not only for me but for the Body of Christ. That's why I keep saying them, and that's why they keep working for me in abundance.

Some people are lazy. They'll say, "Money cometh" when they hear me preach or when they're in some service with a group of believers. But when they're by themselves, they won't say it. That's why they're not getting any money!

If you say, "Money cometh" and believe it in your heart, taking it as a revelation, money will run you down! Those words are packed with the power of God.

Take Hold of the Anointed Word of God To Meet Your Every Need

You see, there is an anointing on those words "Money cometh!" Actually, that word "cometh" just grabs and encompasses everything you need. When something is prophetic, it brings power. It starts a supernatural "turbo" in your circumstances. If you're a single lady, you could say, "Husband cometh!" (And sometimes, *money* cometh because *husband* cometh!)

A single lady might say, "Money cometh!" from the depths of her heart or spirit. And God might say, "She needs something else too. I'm going to give her a husband — and I'm going to give her the money too!" When a word is from God, it produces a *multiplicity* of blessings.

Now how do you change from an echo to a voice? If you have been quoting the Word and not getting any results, how do you make that change over to being a voice?

The first thing you have to do is to admit that you're an echo — that you haven't been abiding in the Word properly and that you haven't allowed it to abide in you through study and meditation. You have to admit it to yourself and to God. You don't have to tell anybody else. You just have to say to yourself, "I've just been echoing. I don't really have a voice. I haven't been speaking like I know I should speak."

Some people are so "spiritual" that they don't want to admit something like that. But if they would admit it, they would be on their way to having a voice. If they are just pretending to have a voice, they can forget ever walking in the fullness of God.

The abiding Word will produce something in your life. It produces results! It will produce the spirit of faith, which releases the sword of the Spirit. The sword releases the authority, ability, weight, and power of God on your behalf. And results will be forthcoming.

The Abiding Word Carries Weight in the Spirit Realm

Look at Luke 4:32 in the *Amplified Bible* again: "And they were amazed at His teaching, for His word was with authority and ability and weight and power." Do you know what it means by "weight"? You know, in the natural, a certain person could walk into a particular organization, and you could tell if he carries a different "weight" or authority from the other people in that organization. For example, if Rev. Kenneth E. Hagin walked into a room full of ministers, almost everyone there would know he carries a different weight. We "boys" would just step aside and let the prophet on through! We'd know that we don't carry the weight, spiritually speaking, that he does. So we'd say, "Go ahead, Brother Hagin; you go first."

Also, by way of illustration, when you're dealing with heavyweights and lightweights in boxing, the lightweight had better yield to the heavyweight! That's why there are different levels in boxing. You don't just put a lightweight in the ring with a heavyweight. If you did, the fight would be over before you knew it!

Don't Be a Spiritual Lightweight

Well, as you meditate in the Word, and as the Word abides in you, you can become a lightweight, a middleweight, or a heavyweight in the spirit realm. It's up to you which one you're going to be. Through meditation, you are letting the Word have weight when you speak it!

I told you, this is a personal thing. In other words, no one can meditate on the Word and abide in the Word for you. You can't say, "Well, I believe I'll just let Sister So-and-so abide for me." It's not going to work! Sister So-and-so's abiding in the Word will help *her*, but it won't help *you*. You must put personal effort into abiding in the Word for *yourself*.

Actually, you need to meditate in the Word every morning, even if you have to get up a little early to do it. So get up out of bed and abide! When you have prayed and prepared yourself spiritually in the morning, it doesn't make any difference what kind of "bug" or problem comes along. It doesn't make any difference to you. You'll just say, "I know who's causing this, and you have to obey me. Devil, get out of here!"

The most precious prize we have in life is the Word of God. We need to get that Word out of the Book and into our spirits. Then it can become the sword of the Spirit. It can become a part of you and produce authority, ability, weight, and power! In other words, the words you say can have the power within them to cause what you say to come to pass!

Say that out loud: "My words have authority, ability, weight, and power!"

You know, some people's word in the natural carries some weight, because they are known for keeping their word. Their words have weight; there is some power behind what they say, because they always back up their words with action.

How much more weight does the Word of the Living God carry! God's Word has *weight*. He always backs up His Word. His Word is heavy enough to get the job done!

Look again at Luke 4:32. I want you to read it like you've never seen it before.

LUKE 4:32
32 And they were astonished at his [Jesus] doctrine: for his word was with power.

I tell you, God recently showed me some things from this verse that caused me to jump, kick, and shout, "Glory to God!" I'd probably read this verse a thousand times before. (You know, it always amazes me; just about the time you think you're a real student of the Word, you find out how much you still have to learn.)

I want to show you something in Luke 4:32 that I had never seen before in this verse. It says, *"And they were astonished at his doctrine* [or teaching]*: for his word was with power* [or authority, ability, weight, and power]*."* Now what did that verse say — that Jesus' word was with power because He was a good orator? Because He had a good command of the language? Because He had a grammar major? No! They were amazed at His teaching, for His word was with *authority*, *ability*, *weight*, and *power*.

Well, I wonder why they were so astonished? This verse is talking about the religious folks, the folks who didn't have any rhema. When folks don't have any rhema, they don't understand when somebody speaks out a rhema.

When folks are echoing, they don't understand a voice. A

voice astonishes them. And to the religious folks who heard Jesus, it was astonishing to hear Someone who spoke like He knew what He was talking about!

Today, it astonishes people to hear a real man or woman of God talking. These people may have been in church all their life, but if they're just an echo, they might have the attitude, *Hey, that person talks like he knows God. He talks like he hangs around with God and has just been in His living room!* They are astonished to hear a voice — to hear the Word of God spoken with power.

That is what I want to emphasize: Jesus' words were with power. And He wants your words to be with power too. Some people do have power in their words, but they can have *more* power.

How Your Words Can Carry Weight in the Spirit Realm

So what does it mean in Luke 4:32 when it says Jesus' Word was with *weight*? I'll illustrate it to you again in the natural. When I walk into my house, I have weight. I have a wife and four children, and because my wife knows what Ephesians 5:22-24 says, she knows that I have the last word in my house. My twenty-one-year-old son, my nineteen-year-old daughter, and my fourteen-year-old son may have plans to go somewhere, but if say, "The direction has changed; you all are going to eat supper with Daddy tonight," they will all start getting on the phone to change their plans and make other arrangements.

Now I wouldn't do that just to be throwing my weight around, but I have the ability to do it, because I have authority in my home, and my words have weight.

The reason some husbands' words don't have any weight at home is, they've got a wagging-tongued wife who doesn't respect the things of God. (Put your stones down; if you're not a wagging tongue, you don't have anything to be upset about!)

I'm illustrating that Jesus' words had weight, and they still do. If you were a single man or woman, and Jesus Christ of Nazareth appeared today, walked up to you, and said, "Tomorrow, you will meet your mate. Prepare thyself," you wouldn't sleep tonight, because His words have weight!

Now, the devil needs to know that you're a heavyweight spiritually — that you have a voice and that your words have weight. He needs to know that you're loaded with the Greater One who lives on the inside of you. He needs to know that. He needs to know that you have the life and ability of God residing on the inside of you. And the only way he can know that fully is if you speak the Word of God with the voice of Jesus. Then when you speak, he not only hears you, but he hears Jesus talking. And when He hears Jesus talking, he'll get to moving!

Supernatural Weight

Jesus never spoke a single time that the devil, demons, or situations didn't obey Him fully. Jesus' words had weight. When you are an echo, your words don't have any weight, because what you're speaking is not the Word in power; it's only a *reflection* of the Word. When you're not meditating on the Word, and the Word is not a rhema to you, it can't be the sword of the Spirit to you. It's when the Word becomes the sword of the Spirit to you that your words will carry supernatural weight that can change any natural situation.

When you speak the Word of God with the voice of Jesus, your words will carry weight! They will carry power, authority, weight, *and* ability.

Did you know that authority and ability are not the same thing? For example, a policeman has authority to stop traffic, but he doesn't have the physical ability within himself to actually force that traffic to stop. Now if someone kept driving when he said to stop, he has some ability on his side in that he has a gun. That gun is his *ability*, but his badge is his *authority*.

When we speak with the voice of Jesus, we have all of that working for us — power, authority, weight, and ability. But when we speak with an echo, we come up short — powerless and empty-handed.

Locate Yourself — Are You an Echo?

Too many Christians are just echoes. They're saying things, but it's really not *in* them. They don't know the difference between a voice and an echo. I want you now to question yourself. You may read your Bible and go to a good church, but I want you to look back at the last ten circumstances you spoke to in your life. Did you speak to them with an echo or a voice? If nine of those things are still on the line, so to speak, or haven't changed the way you need them to change, you've got an echo, not a voice. (I'd say you ought to at least be batting eight-to-two by now!)

To Speak With Authority Is a Sonship Privilege

When you speak with the voice of authority, Heaven is behind you, and what you speak to should obey your voice. Remember, I said a voice has confidence and boldness. A voice will bring you bolt upright and out of your seat, looking at your circumstance in the face and saying, "Did you hear me!"

That's the way you have to talk to the devil. I tell you, Satan will run from a voice. An echo makes a sound, all right, but when you really need something, an echo doesn't produce any power. It doesn't come through for you. But the voice is the real thing. People will come to a voice, but they will not follow an echo. (Some pastors wonder why their church is empty.)

Actually, echoes follow echoes. So numbers don't really always correctly judge whether a church has a voice or not. Echoes like echoes. Echoes want to tell other echoes that they are not living right, because they are not living right themselves. So all the echoes hang out together. Many of them don't even want to hear a voice.

But we must all become a voice if we want to see changes — supernatural changes by God's Spirit.

> **JOHN 11:40**
> 40 Jesus saith unto her [Martha], Said I not unto thee, that, if thou wouldest believe, thou shouldest SEE the glory of God?

Now, when you speak with the voice of Jesus, the *voice* of God will bring on the scene the *glory* of God. The glory of God is the Presence, power, ability, and strength of God. When you speak with the voice of Jesus, the glory and Presence of God can't help Himself — He *must* come to your rescue! Why? Because He heard His Son speak! No, we are not *the* Son of God. But we *are* sons of God.

> **1 JOHN 3:2**
> 2 Beloved, now are we the sons of God, and it doth not yet appear what we shall be: but we know that, when he shall appear, we shall be like him; for we shall see him as he is.

> **ROMANS 8:14**
> 14 For as many as are led by the Spirit of God, they are the sons of God.

We are sons and daughters of God. We have equal rights with Jesus in the Kingdom. He gave that privilege to us. We are heirs of God and joint heirs with Jesus Christ (Rom. 8:17). What Christ did when He was ministering on the earth, you can do too. I'm talking about operating with power, authority, weight, and ability in your life. I'm not talking about just being a church member; I'm talking about walking in the truth of God's Word where it's joy unspeakable and full of glory!

Let's continue reading in John 11.

JOHN 11:41
41 Then they took away the stone from the place where the dead was laid. And Jesus lifted up his eyes, and said, Father, I thank thee that thou hast heard me.

Notice the last part of this verse, because this is the voice speaking: ". . . *Jesus lifted up his eyes, and said, Father, I THANK THEE THAT THOU HAST HEARD ME.*"

In other words, Jesus said, "I know I already have what I am about to say, because I have it in here, in My heart. When I speak it out, it's only going to be a demand that what I already possess come to pass in this realm."

Get Full of the Word and Then Thank God That He Has Heard You!

Think about something you're dealing with right now. Think about something that's hindering you and holding you back from getting where you want to be. Get the Word of God into your heart and say, "Father, I thank You that You have heard me," and you count the matter as solved.

There is more to that passage of Scripture in John 11. Look at verse 42.

JOHN 11:42
42 And I KNEW THAT THOU HEAREST ME ALWAYS: but because of the people which stand by I said it, that they may believe that thou hast sent me.

Wait a minute now — what does "always" mean? It means *all the time*. He didn't say, "Father, I *think* you always hear Me." Or, "I *hope* You always hear Me." Or, "I *wish* You'd always hear Me"! No! Jesus said, ". . . *I KNEW that thou hearest me always: but because of the people which stand by I said it, that they may believe that thou hast sent me.*"

JOHN 11:43
43 And when he thus had spoken, he cried with a loud voice, Lazarus, come forth.

That is the example of a voice, not an echo! I mean, Jesus told that boy out there in that tomb to come out. You know for yourself that in the natural, if you were to call one of your children by name to come to you, he or she should come running. If you said, "Charles, come here," who should come to you? *Charles* should come to you! Well, spiritual things come to you in the same way. When you call them with a voice, they come forth!

Notice when Jesus "thus had spoken," He cried with a loud *voice*, "Lazarus, come forth!" If Jesus had been down there in that graveyard with an echo, Lazarus would still be in that grave today. But the glory of God came when Jesus spoke, because He spoke with a voice. And the Presence, strength, and power of God came and pulled Lazarus out of the grave!

JOHN 11:44
44 And he that was dead came forth, bound hand and foot with graveclothes: and his face was bound about with a napkin. Jesus saith unto them, Loose him, and let him go.

How do we know Jesus was a voice and not an echo? Because His words were with authority, ability, weight, and power! When He spoke, things *happened*! Jesus got results when He spoke, because He spoke with a *voice*.

I am so glad I know who I am — are you? Sure, you are going to be persecuted in this life. Sure, you are going to have tests and trials, but that doesn't mean anything if you know how to speak the Word of God with the voice of Jesus!

You see, God speaks to us when we are dealing with things as we read the Word and love Him. God gives us a direct word from the Bible to deal directly with the situation we are currently facing. Then that Word becomes a sword of the Spirit.

Stale Manna and a Dull Sword

I believe that many times, we are dealing with stale manna and a dull sword! But, you see, the Holy Ghost wants to deal with that problem afresh for you. That's why I don't just automatically think I have the scripture I need when I am dealing with something. I don't just start quoting scriptures I know. No, I look to the Lord. I pray in tongues and open my Bible. And when I get to a certain scripture, it seems like it just leaps out at me. I close my Bible. I don't need fifty-five more scriptures. When the Spirit of God and the anointing come upon you, you turn into another person. You turn into a "superman"!

I told you we've got too many "Clark Kents" in the Church. They're running around in the flesh. They need to go into their closet and come out as "Superman." They need to go in there with the Word and get anointed! I tell you, when a person senses the anointing of God upon him, there is nothing that can stop him — absolutely nothing! When you get that mighty-moving force of the Word of God on the inside of you, you are unstoppable!

The Word Works Inside Out!

The Word works on the inside of you so you can speak it out in faith on the outside — to your circumstances. And that to which you speak must obey you.

But it takes time. That's why Jesus said, *"If ye abide in me, and my words abide in you, ye shall ask what ye will, and it shall be done unto you"* (John 15:7). Jesus is saying, "If you abide in the Living Word, and the written Word abides in you...."

Jesus is the *Living Word*. The "logos" is the *written Word*. The Bible, the written Word, was written by men divinely inspired by the Holy Ghost. Abided in, the written Word becomes a supernatural force in your life. If you meditate in the written Word and have fellowship with the Living Word, then you can start talking to circumstances, and they will obey you. (That should excite you and make you shout!)

But, as I said, nobody else can do this for you; you have to do it for yourself. You have to spend time with Jesus. You have to have a certain intimacy with Him through His Word. And, much like a wife becomes pregnant through intimacy with her husband, you become "pregnant" with the Word because you have spent so much time with it that it is "conceived" on the inside of you — in your spirit — and produces life.

John 15:7 in the *Amplified Bible* gives us a little more insight.

> **JOHN 15:7**
> 7 If you live in Me [abide vitally united to Me] and My words remain in you and continue to live in you, in your hearts, ask whatever you will and it shall be done for you.

So feed upon the written Word; have a conversation with the Living Word. Then when your rhema comes and you speak it out, that spoken Word will have power. That power is the result of a combination of the Presence of the Living Word and the written Word in your heart. That's why Jesus said, "If you abide in Me. . . ." In other words, "If you spend time with and have fellowship with Me and allow My words to abide in you, then go ahead and make a demand on what is legally yours. It will have to obey you, because you learned to speak with a voice!"

Anyone Can Get in Position
To Speak With a Voice

What I am teaching is for anyone in the Body of Christ who will receive it. God is blessing me because I'm telling people about the righteous acts of God (Judges 5:11; 1 Sam. 12:7). I'm rehearsing what God is doing in my life to be an example for the Body of Christ. I'm not bragging on me; I'm bragging on Jesus. I am what I am because He is who He is, and I've made a connection with Him properly; therefore, I am blessed.

We who are in the Body of Christ are washed in the blood of Jesus — no matter who we are. We are neither male nor female, Jew nor Greek (Col. 3:11). We are all one in the Body of Christ. Yes, we are different colors. Some of us are shaded lighter than others, but it doesn't make any difference. What matters is that we're born again, washed in the blood of the Lamb and speaking the Word of God with the voice of Jesus.

Books and Tape Series By Dr. Leroy Thompson:

How To Speak the Word of God With the Voice of Jesus
192-page book $10.95 + $2.00 s/h
Money Cometh to the Body of Christ!
313 pages $13.95 + $2.00 s/h
The ABC's of Framing Your World With the Word of God
114 pages $6.95 + $2.00 s/h
How To Speak the Word of God With the Voice of Jesus
(4-audiotape series) $20.00 + $2.00 s/h
Money Cometh to the Body of Christ! Vol. 1
(8 audiotapes) $40.00 + $2.00 s/h
Money Cometh to the Body of Christ! Vol. 2
(8 audiotapes) $40.00 + $2.00 s/h
How To Have Faith for Miracles
(6 audiotapes) $30.00 + $2.00 s/h
The Power of Agreement in Marriage
(3 audiotapes) $15.00 + $2.00 s/h
Legal Weapons Against Sickness and Disease
(4 audiotapes) $20.00 + $2.00 s/h
100% Victory Over the Tongue
(3 audiotapes) $15.00 + $2.00 s/h

How To Order:

Call 1-504-473-8874 for Visa/MasterCard orders
Or
Mail check or money order to Ever Increasing Word Ministries
(Allow 4-5 weeks for delivery.)

To receive a FREE catalog of Dr. Thompson's teaching materials or to receive a FREE quarterly newsletter from this ministry, write to:

**Ever Increasing Word Ministries
P. O. Box 7
Darrow, LA 70725**